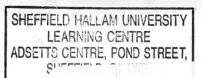

101

D1100527

PRO**…**HE
BEAUTIFUL FRAME

A History of the Sheffield, Peak District
& South Yorkshire Branch of the
Council for the Protection of Rural England

Melvyn Jones

The **Hallamshire** Press
2001

© 2001 Melvyn Jones and the CPRE, Sheffield, Peak District & South Yorkshire Branch

Published by The Hallamshire Press in association with the Sheffield, Peak District & South Yorkshire Branch of the Council for the Protection of Rural England

The Hallamshire Press Limited
134 Archer Road
Sheffield S8 0JZ

Typeset by The Hallamshire Press Limited, Sheffield
Printed by The Cromwell Press, Trowbridge, Wiltshire

British Library Cataloguing in Publication Data:
   A catalogue record for this book is available from the British Library

ISBN 1 874718 61 X

Looking eastwards from Upper Hurst farm towards Birley Edge in the summer of 2000. Birley Edge was one of the areas north-west of the built-up area of Sheffield included in the Branch's map of green belt recommendations presented to Sheffield Corporation in 1937. Sixty-five acres of land on and around Birley Edge were acquired by Alderman J.G. Graves and presented to the City of Sheffield in 1941. (Joan Jones)

Contents

Foreword
By Sir Chris Bonington

It is my great pleasure to write the Foreword for this book. What is now the Sheffield, Peak District and South Yorkshire Branch of the CPRE was from the very start the pace-setter and model for local environmental organisations in every part of the country to follow. And as Melvyn Jones emphasises, the Branch has campaigned for more than three-quarters of a century with sharp focus and undeviating high principle, including for two years before the CPRE as a national organisation came into existence.

Whatever else is forgotten, the Branch will go down in history as a major force in environmental conservation because of the achievement of its two 'grand purposes': the designation of a national park in the Peak District and the creation of a permanent Sheffield Green Belt. But there were so many more equally successful campaigns in the wider countryside and the urban fringe that the reader gasps with admiration. And at the head of this crusading society for so long, the tireless, single-minded, and selfless Ethel and Gerald Haythornthwaite were without parallel. Ethel's ability to persuade and influence and Gerald's grasp of technical detail over a wide area of disciplines made them formidable opponents and splendid allies.

We shall not see the likes of Ethel and Gerald again. They were of their time and their creative partnership was unique. Today we live in an age of narrow specialisms and expertise, but experts come in all sorts of shapes and from all kinds of origins and one of the key roles of the officers of the Branch in the new century will be to orchestrate the army of volunteer experts who can make such a huge contribution to protecting the countryside when operating within a sharply focused campaigning organisation. The book will encourage and stimulate all those who live in the Peak District, Sheffield and the rest of South Yorkshire to carry on the fight for the countryside into the twenty-first century—and beyond. I wish this timely book and the Branch every success.

Author's Preface

In October 1996 I was invited informally to 22a Endcliffe Crescent to look at the archive material built up over more than 70 years in connection with the work of the CPRE, Sheffield, Peak District and South Yorkshire Branch, and to give my opinion of its value.

It took only a very short time for me to realise that it was of great significance on three counts: it was a detailed record of the pioneering work of the Branch in protecting the local countryside and in shaping thinking about landscape conservation in the region; it recorded not only what the Branch did, but also how it did it—a combination of vision, unshakable principle, meticulous research, rational argument, dedication, doggedness and, not least, by the devotion and generosity of its ordinary members; it also demonstrated the unique roles played by Ethel and Gerald Haythornthwaite.

I concluded that the archive ought to be carefully preserved and properly catalogued. I also suggested that it would be a wholly appropriate project for the archive to be used as the basis for a properly researched and illustrated book about the history of the Branch and the pioneering work of the Haythornthwaites. It would be a fitting testimonial to their pioneering efforts and long-lasting influence—and also to their generosity. The book ought to be seen as a vehicle for inspiring the Branch to continue its campaigning unabated into the next century.

Preliminary cataloguing of the archive was quickly completed and the Executive Committee decided to commission a book about the history of the Branch based on the documentary archive. I was delighted to be selected—following invitations to various local authors to respond to a project brief—to undertake the researching and writing of the book.

When I responded to the project brief, I said that working out the detailed organisation of the book would be part of the research process, but would be partly chronological and partly thematic. The book would be an appropriate weaving together of the development of the work of the Branch and the lives and contributions of the Haythornthwaites. I said I also wanted to convey the continuity of principled campaigning and lobbying, with no issue too small, producing the constant flow of pressure which resulted in the powerful and sustained conservation voice that is the CPRE, Sheffield, Peak District and South Yorkshire Branch. I wanted to convey an ethos and a stance as well as to record events.

This book is the result. I have attempted to write a readable text based largely on the original documents in the Branch archive collection: minutes of Executive Meetings; annual reports; memoranda; case notes; evidence to public inquiries; maps; correspondence—official and personal; the personal papers of the Haythornthwaites; all Branch publications; Gerald's speeches and published articles; press cuttings; and the enormous collection of glass lantern slides and 35mm transparencies, a tiny selection of which I have used to illustrate the text.

I have also been helped enormously by the following individuals who have granted me interviews and/or answered innumerable queries for which I express my gratitude: Narendra Bajaria, Roy Bullen, Jack Burling, Lynn Crowe, Elizabeth Garland, Margaret Gray, the late Arthur Humphrey, Ted Spencer, and most of all, Jean Smart. I have also had access to a long taped interview between Gerald and Fiona Reynolds in 1988 (when she was National Director of CPRE) in which he reviewed his career and the work of the Branch in some detail. This 'from the horse's mouth' testimony was of outstanding value. I must also thank Shirley Foster for liaising between myself, the Branch and the publisher and giving enthusiastic support throughout the project. Last but not least I wish to thank my wife Joan for her forbearance and help while the book was being researched, written and edited.

1

The foundation years

1924–1929

I

ON 7 MAY 1924 A SMALL AND SELECT GATHERING of like-minded men and women, disturbed by the increasing defacement of the beauty of the Peak District by 'incongruous and promiscuous development', met at Endcliffe Vale House in the quiet western suburbs of Sheffield. They had come together to discuss the possible formation of a society for the preservation of local scenery. The only formal business conducted at that meeting was the discussion preceding the decision to form such a society, although strong feelings were expressed against a proposed new motor road through the Winnats and it was arranged that the newly appointed Honorary Secretary should write about this to the National Trust.

The founder-members present at the first meeting were a cross-section of Sheffield's leading citizens mainly from industrial, academic and professional backgrounds: Mrs Ethel Gallimore; Mr H.B.S. Gibbs, architect; Miss Moorwood; Rev. Martin Pope; Dr W.S. Porter, physician and local historian (who took the chair); Miss Porter; Mr Somerset; Mr G.H.B. Ward, representing ramblers' interests; Gertrude Ward (Mrs Gallimore's sister); Alan Ward (her brother); and Mr W.R. White. Invited but unable to attend were T. Walter Hall, the antiquary and archivist; Mr and Mrs Samuel Osborn; and Mr Carus Wilson. In his absence Sir Henry Hadow, the Vice-Chancellor of Sheffield University, was proposed and seconded as president.

The Honorary Secretary elected at the initial meeting was Mrs Ethel Gallimore who had not only instigated the meeting but had provided the accommodation for the meeting at the home of her mother. Ethel Gallimore, founder, inspiration, and prime mover of the fledgling society was the daughter of T.W. Ward, the Sheffield industrialist. Little could she have known what wheels she was setting in motion and what achievements

Ethel Mary Bassett Ward aged 21. From a portrait in oils.

Endcliffe Vale House, Sheffield, the Ward family home and office of the Branch from 1924 until 1956.

would have been gained by the time of her death more than 60 years later. Widowed during the Great War, and now 30 years old, she threw all her energy, and her genius for influencing and persuading, into the pioneering venture. At a 'lantern' lecture given in 1945 she expounded movingly on what the countryside around Sheffield, especially in the Peak District, meant to her and how its gradual loss had affected her:

> *Some of you must stand in the same relation to Sheffield as myself. At least if you were not born and bred here, you have spent a large part of your lives in the district; so that the city and its surroundings seem to belong to us—or we belong to them. Some of you may be newcomers, and would probably answer like most newcomers when one asks them how they like Sheffield: 'Well, it's a good place to get out of'. As Ruskin said, 'An ugly picture in a beautiful frame'.*
>
> *My childhood impressions of the city were—a gloomy noisy shapeless phenomenon: but outside the city—there one began to live. The escape into clean air, the gradual return to nature; with this came satisfaction and peace. Broken streams through woods and meadows, upland pastures and stone farms, the primaeval wildness of the moors.*
>
> *Redmires or Ringinglow meant freedom, Owler Bar, then unspoilt, the solitude of the moorland scene, the crags of Moscar or Stanage excitement, the outline of Winhill something to worship. The starved townchild's reaction to natural life. But, whatever it was it might be better not to be, than only to know the sterility of the industrial city, <u>without</u> nature beyond. One grew to become conscious of its profounder value, something beyond health and high spirits. And along with this came the sickening realisation, as the ugly suburbs straggled out and the farms disappeared, that it was all going. But a helpless uneasiness may be replaced by action, and now some who comprehend the significance of Sheffield's surroundings to her citizens, spend a large part of their lives trying to save them.*

But looking back and philosophising was not the order of the day in 1924. The immediate task before the founder-members was to identify specific goals and to find a *modus operandi*. And to decide what to call themselves. The latter took much longer to resolve than finding work to undertake and the means to do that work.

At the first meeting proper of the new society on 8 October 1924, under the chairmanship of Dr William Porter, the first decision made was to rescind the resolutions of the preliminary meeting in May, and to call themselves a committee not a society. They also resolved to ask the National Trust if they could be allowed to call themselves 'The Sheffield & District Vigilance Committee of the National Trust'. The first of these decisions was in turn rescinded at the next meeting in July 1925 and it was resolved to call the society 'The Sheffield Association for the Protection of Local Scenery'. In December 1926 the Honorary Secretary attended the inaugural meeting of the Council for the Preservation of Rural England and at the Association's next meeting in February 1927 an invitation to become affiliated to the CPRE was unanimously accepted. But the Association continued to work under its own name for the next three years.

II

From the outset, the multi-faceted strategy that was to be the hallmark of the society throughout the rest of the century was put into operation: gathering compelling evidence, lobbying, persuading, educating opinion, and, where practicable, purchasing land to take it out of the development process. The society also learnt at a very early stage how time-consuming the work would be, how the onus would be continually thrown back on them, and how important it was to grind down officialdom. For example, the minutes of the Committee meeting in October 1927 records that two members of the Association, at the suggestion of the Town Clerk of Sheffield, had made a tour 'of the rural districts within the city boundary with the result that a list of areas where [disfiguring] advertisements might be prohibited had been drawn up...' Many years later at one of her slide lectures, Ethel expanded ruefully on this bald statement:

> *After we had badgered him a good deal, the City Surveyor at that time, asked us to do a job. 'You people' he said 'are pressing us to prevent rural areas being spoilt by advertisements. Will you make recommendations as to where these should not be allowed?' Being rather green, and eager to be employed, we immediately consented, and quickly discovered the astuteness of the official. It took every afternoon for four months to make the detailed survey required.*
>
> *This piece of work, together with a map, was duly presented to the City Council...and duly shelved. It took seven years to get the Council to take action on our Report...*

The Mayfield Valley.

The 1920s were an age of modernisation: car ownership was increasing rapidly, and the middle classes had discovered touring and day tripping, and the charabanc outing was increasingly popular; growing numbers of car owners were also keen to leave the central parts of cities and relocate in the rural fringes and in villages in the wider countryside; amenities were also spreading from town to countryside—piped water supplies, electricity and telephones; and modern industry using rural resources was expanding rapidly. These changes brought many threats to the countryside—road widening, bridge replacement, hotel and 'roadhouse' building; intrusive billboards, village expansion and suburban sprawl, reservoir construction, unsightly electricity pylons and telegraph poles, quarries and factory chimneys, and uncontrolled tipping and a rapidly increasing litter problem. There was no planning legislation to prohibit or curb the worst excesses of incompatible developments and appropriate bye-laws were lacking or insufficiently stringently enforced to deter minor infringements and nuisances. In the early years the Association lobbied for the preparation and implementation of adequate Town and Country Planning Schemes.

Members of the new Association were fully alive to all the threats to the local rural scenery, and this awareness is reflected in the developments or proposed developments in the local countryside that preoccupied them in the first six years of the Association's existence. The proposed construction of a motor road through the Winnats Pass was the subject of discussion at the very first meeting and assurances were sought periodically from the Ministry of Transport that permission had not been given for such a development, in order to ensure that sufficient time was available to assemble a case for an alternative route if necessary. As traffic densities and vehicle weights increased, the possible demolition of old bridges was also of concern and this prompted discussion at one of the early meetings of the rumoured plan to demolish the medieval bridge in Rotherham. The building of new bridges in modern materials out of keeping with the rural areas in which they were located also caused concern—cases in point being a proposed new steel suspension bridge at the stepping stones near Offerton and a proposed new concrete bridge for charabanc traffic near Tissington. In late 1926 the Secretary arranged with the Society for the Protection of Ancient Buildings (SPAB) that all the bridges worth preserving in the Peak District would be scheduled in the following spring. By the following May she was able to report that SPAB had listed all the bridges which were considered necessary to be scheduled by the Office of Works.

The existence of disfiguring advertisements, disfiguring because of their intrusiveness and their strident colours, and the tardiness of both Derbyshire County Council and Sheffield City Council in either introducing bye-laws (Sheffield) or applying them rigorously (Derbyshire) was a regular item of discussion at Committee meetings, usually followed by representations, letters and, as we have already seen, in the case of Sheffield, a detailed survey and set of recommendations. Strident colours were also complained about in the case of the 'incongruous colours' of the new police boxes which had appeared at the rural boundaries of Sheffield in 1928 and the Secretary was instructed to write to the Chief Constable suggesting green paint instead of red and cream. At the next meeting it was reported that the City Architect agreed with the Association that the boxes should be painted green or some colour that would not jar with the surroundings, but just in case he forgot, a member of the Committee agreed to remind him of his promise to this effect. Petrol stations, again often garishly painted and out of harmony with local building styles and materials, were also subject to close scrutiny.

The River Derwent near Hathersage. (Phil Barnes)

Disfiguring advertisement in the 1920s at Hope. (Phil Barnes)

Industrial expansion in the Peak District, small in scale and isolated as it was in the 1920s, was a matter that concerned the new society, but compared to the threat of residential expansion it was a relatively uncommon agenda item at meetings during the first six years. Quarrying between Ladybower and Cut-Throat Bridge had been noticed in 1924 and it was agreed that more information was needed about the development. But among industrial issues, for the rest of the 1920s it was the new Hope Valley Cement Works that occupied most of the Committee's time. It was first discussed in May 1927, before the works was built, when two members of the Association were asked to find out more about the proposed development. At the October meeting of the Association a letter of advice was read to members from the CPRE, whose representative had had an interview with the engineer of the Works. The minutes of the meeting record that

> *It was decided that opposition to the erection of the works would be useless, but as the firm seemed reasonably disposed, certain concessions to scenery might be demanded. With a view to this the secretary was asked to get in touch with the Chapel-en-le-Frith council, and certain members of the Association agreed to accept the invitation of Messrs Earle Ltd to see the plans and site of the works at Hope.*

At the March meeting in 1928, a report was made about the visit to inspect the site and plans, but the minutes are silent about the Works itself, and concern was only expressed about railway bridges for the Works and the fear that the wires and supports for the electricity supply would be a disfigurement. The first Annual Report, covering the years 1924–31, noted that the firm, at the Committee's request, had taken considerable trouble to keep their buildings and bridges in keeping with the character of the district and had seeded banks and planted a large number of trees.

In the absence of controlling legislation, village expansion and suburban sprawl were the subject of much debate and not a little frustration. At the Committee meeting held in February 1927 the development of land between the village of Great Longstone and the railway station was discussed and it was arranged that the owners of the land should be approached 'with a view to testing their interest in keeping the new building in harmony with the traditional style of the village, this being of local stone.' At the same meeting a proposed scheme for more than 1,000 houses at Coal Aston on land owned by Sheffield Corporation and Norton Rural District Council, and about which little was known, was also discussed briefly. At the next meeting in May it was reported that the proposed house building scheme at Great Longstone was unlikely to proceed at present, but in the case of Coal Aston, the Town Clerk of Sheffield had given his opinion that the housing scheme 'was too far ahead for consideration.'

Housing schemes were also on the agenda at the last meeting of 1927 when a proposed scheme at Norton was discussed and it was agreed to approach the agent and owner of the land about the likelihood of obtaining a restriction on the type of buildings that could be erected. By March 1928 a meeting had taken place between the chairman of the Association and Mr Gleeson, the house builder, and the latter 'had agreed to build in harmony with the character of the present village as far as possible.' The Chairman was asked to press the matter further and ask for the employment of an architect.

Most disturbing of all was not a case of village expansion or suburban infilling, but the possible building of houses in a valued piece of countryside on the edge of Sheffield—at Blacka Moor to the south of the A625 to the south-west of Dore. This 448 acre site with majestic views of moorland and woodland was part of the Duke of Rutland's estate that was put on the market in 1927 and had been acquired privately for building development. The possible use of this site for building speculation was discussed for the first time, and at length, at the Committee meeting held in May 1928, and it was resolved to ask Norton Rural District Council to receive a deputation from the Association on the matter. At the next meeting in October a petition (the word 'memorial' was used) to Norton Rural District Council compiled by the Chairman, by then Dr R.G. Abercrombie (Dr Porter having resigned in May 1926 and died in 1927), was read out and approved. The memorial urged that Blacka Moor should be scheduled under the Norton Town Planning Scheme as an open space where building was prohibited. Norton Council was sympathetic and invited a deputation from the Association to discuss the matter further. In January 1929 it was reported that 'hopeful negotiations' were taking place. The area was indeed designated that year as a 'private open space' in which building was prohibited, but the new owner announced his intention to fight the designation and the matter was not resolved until 1933.

Geographically more distant but equally worrying was the proposed Stockport Waterworks Scheme in the Goyt Valley which came onto the agenda for the first time in October 1929. A resolution from the Buxton Branch of the Derbyshire Council for the Preservation of the Countryside protesting about the scheme was read out and it was resolved to send a similar resolution to Stockport Corporation. Representations about this particular development were to rumble on into the 1930s.

The spread of electric power and electric lighting out of towns across the countryside was another potential source of landscape disfigurement in the Peak District. Uncontrolled development would mean massive intrusion of wires and pylons criss-crossing the landscape and spoiling skylines. The first general discussion of this potential problem took place in March 1928 and the Secretary was requested to write to Derbyshire County Council for information and to the CPRE for advice. At the October meeting it was reported that the CPRE was still negotiating with the Electricity Commissioners about the question and had suggested that the Association try to obtain plans of the proposed schemes in the Peak District. Meanwhile it was noted that the district councils at Chapel-en-le-Frith and Whaley Bridge had both objected to overhead cables in their areas.

In early 1929 the Central Electricity Board assured the Association that none of the main transmission lines would pass through the Peak District and this was confirmed by close inspection of the Mid-East England and North-West England schemes. However, the Association had been informed that the Yorkshire Electric Power Company was shortly to erect a double line of overhead cables from Barnsley to the Cement Works at Hope, via Bolsterstone, Ewden Valley, Moscar and Bamford Edge. A deputation from the Association met representatives of Yorkshire Electric, but it was reported in May 1929 that although discussions were friendly and suggested route deviations had been considered, after months of negotiation the company had reported that it had been unable to arrange for any of the suggested deviations because of the intransigence of landowners. But there was also some good news to report: the Derby & Notts Power Company, which was supplying power to Eyam and Hathersage, had agreed, on the recommendation of the Association, to place its lines underground for half a mile between Grindleford Bridge and Padley Brook, thus saving the disfigurement of a beautiful riverside walk.

Two other smaller-scale, but nevertheless critically important problems, were continually re-visited in Committee discussions in the first six years: uncontrolled tipping and the problem of litter. Tipping was seen as a visual problem and as a danger to healthy river systems. Almost from the outset the proposal by a firm of builders and contractors to use the valley near Grindleford station as a tip was a focus of attention and a 'watching brief' established. Once tipping began, great efforts were made to persuade those responsible (it was reported to be used mainly by Sheffield Corporation) to discontinue tipping there, but without success. The general subject of riverside rubbish tips, particularly along the Derwent, was introduced by the Chairman in December 1926 and it was decided to send a letter to the Clerk of Bakewell Council protesting against the defilement of rivers in this way. At the May 1927 meeting specific examples of riverside-tips were named at Bamford, Baslow, Beeley and Hope. By the beginning of October 1927 it was reported that riverside tipping at Baslow and Hope had been prohibited.

Littering was attacked by direct approaches to organisations. Bus, tram and railway companies were asked to put up notices in their vehicles requesting passengers not to drop litter in the countryside, and to incorporate such notices in their timetables. This met with success, but in thanking the Tramways Committee in December 1926, it was requested that a more conspicuous notice be introduced when their new country routes timetables were published. Sheffield headteachers were also written to and requested to address their pupils about dropping litter and starting fires. And the motoring organisations were also approached about circulating a leaflet about litter in their handbooks.

There was also the issue of getting their message across to the general public and getting the support of the population at large. A major opportunity to mount a professionally-looking exhibition arose when the loan of the 'Save the Countryside' Exhibition, which had originally been held in Leicester at the Preservation of the Countryside conference in October 1928, was offered to Sheffield. It was decided to hold it if possible in the Cutlers' Hall with a supplementary local exhibition alongside the national exhibition. Suitable speakers were to be invited, the Lord Mayor would be invited to open the exhibition, and it would be widely advertised. After one postponement, the exhibition eventually took place between 19–26 September 1929 at the Cutlers' Hall. It was hailed as a great success. It attracted about 4,000 visitors in addition to children from the top two standards of local elementary schools —about 800 a day—who were addressed by members of the Association and others. The exhibition was opened by Professor Patrick Abercrombie, town planner (he was the author of the Sheffield Civic Survey) and Secretary of the CPRE. He criticised central government, local authorities, the Forestry Commission, electricity companies and private individuals for disfiguring the countryside, but also pointed out that it was 'easier to curse than to praise' and that it would be a sad thing if the movement were to preserve the countryside 'like a stuffed specimen in a museum. The more the country is used the better.' Other speakers at the opening were Sir Henry Hadow and H.H. Peach who had organised the original exhibition on behalf of the CPRE in Leicester. The Master Cutler presided at a lantern lecture given by Clough Williams-Ellis. The national exhibition was mounted around the walls of the hall and the local exhibition occupied the centre. A particularly striking exhibit in the local section was a glass case filled with what the *Sheffield Daily Telegraph* described as 'an indescribable heap of filthy paper, empty fruit tins, broken mineral bottles, cigarette and chocolate wrappers, matchboxes, cigarette ends, as well as other litter'. The exhibit was labelled 'What Sheffield left at Stanage last Bank Holiday'.

The local exhibition 'of local scenery and disfigurement' adopted the 'cautionary tale' method which was to become the hallmark of the Branch's approach to its public relations activity for many years to come: before and after, the right and the wrong, the beautiful and the ugly. The *Sheffield Daily Telegraph* announced that it was 'impressed by the sagacity with which it [the exhibition] has been devised…The method is to show not only how things are done wrong, but how they can be done right.' In an article specially written by Ethel for the *Sheffield Daily Telegraph* before the opening of the exhibition, she wrote that the organising committee had been working for many months to bring home to Sheffielders the dangers that threatened the local countryside 'in some striking pictorial form'. In this the Committee succeeded brilliantly, one of the most reported and privately and publicly discussed aspects of the local exhibition being the masterly use of photography.

One newspaper pointed out that the local photographs were the work of a local amateur photographer. The photographer in question was Philip Barnes, or as Clough Williams-Ellis called him in a letter to Ethel 'your very gifted Mr Barnes'. Phil Barnes, a draughtsman, and keen rambler with an intimate knowledge of the Peak District, had been elected to the Committee in 1928. His photographic skills were to be put to more permanent use in the future.

The local exhibition was praised by the CPRE, went on show at the National Conference for the Preservation of the Countryside in Manchester in October, and arrangements made for it to be shown at Chesterfield and Buxton. In fact it ran and ran for several years all over the Peak District.

Win Hill from Kinder Scout. (Phil Barnes)

III

The crowning achievement of the early years was the purchase of Longshaw Lodge and its grounds on 29 September 1927. The Longshaw Lodge estate was the property of the Duke of Rutland. It comprised the Duke's shooting lodge, a formal garden and park, woodlands and farms amounting to 747 acres, together with surrounding high moorlands covering a further 10,786 acres. The entire property was put up for auction without restrictions in 1927.

The local authorities of Sheffield and Chesterfield resolved to acquire most of the high moorlands for water catchment purposes and, through the good offices of Sheffield City Council, a Joint Committee of the Association and the Sheffield Council of Social Service was able to purchase the lodge and its grounds. This was accomplished by the purchase of Longshaw Lodge and the surrounding 747 acres by Sheffield City Council who then conveyed the property to the Joint Committee upon payment of £13,000 raised by a bank overdraft.

Longshaw scenery.

Within five months over £9,000 had been raised, largely as the result of generous gifts by members of the Association and by the Sheffield Town Trustees. Additional funds were raised by two public appeals, in which the Sheffield Ramblers' Association played an important part, and by a further donation from Sheffield Town Trustees. The payment of the outstanding amount of £1,339 was made by the National Trust. The Longshaw property was eventually conveyed to the National Trust on 25 March 1931 and publicly handed over to them on 27 June. It was the Trust's first countryside property in the Peak District.

IV

In the first six years of its existence, while finding its feet and finding its voice, the Association had drawn up the battle lines, strategies and tactics that were to sustain it for the rest of the century:

- educating the public about the beauty of the natural and man-made beauty of the Peak District and to the damage being caused by uncontrolled development;
- persuading local authorities, builders and developers to design buildings and choose materials appropriate to their regional and local setting;
- forestalling development by purchasing land;
- pursuing campaigns against and sending petitions to individuals and public and private organisations, relentlessly, and without fear and favour.

2

Consolidation

1930–1935

I

THE FIRST ITEM AT THE FEBRUARY 1930 meeting of the Executive was the announcement that P.A. (Phil) Barnes, who had become a member of the Association in December 1928, had been appointed to the salaried position of Assistant Secretary since the last meeting in October 1929. The minute noted 'that therefore there was every hope that its [the Association's] efficacy would be much increased.' His appointment meant that the mantle of driving business forward could be shared between the Secretary and Assistant Secretary, and Barnes' particular skills of meticulous preparation, presentation, negotiation and photography, and his intimate knowledge of the locality, could be capitalised on. He resigned in 1933 to become Secretary of the Lancashire Branch of the CPRE where he remained until his death in 1966 at the age of 67. He was also leader and founder of the voluntary wardens at Longshaw. His book *Trespassers Will Be Prosecuted* (1934) about lack of access to the wilderness areas in the Peak District is a classic of its kind, illustrated by his fine photographs.

He was succeeded as Assistant Secretary by John V. Worsnip, an architect. Like Phil Barnes, Worsnip stayed for three years during which time he made invaluable contributions to the development of the work of the Peak District Advisory Panel of Architects and with the associated publication *Housing in the Peak District* (1934). He left in October 1935 to take up the position of Senior Assistant to the Peak Joint Planning Committee following the setting up of two planning committees covering Derbyshire, and the appointment of a county planning officer earlier in the year.

The year 1933 saw the first change in the chairmanship for seven years with Professor E.S. Forster taking over from Dr Abercrombie, following the latter's resignation due to the pressure of work. Among new members of the Executive Committee in the 1930–35 period were Professor Joseph Husband who was to be a major figure in resisting another attempt to build a major road through the Winnats at the end of the 1930s, and Dr John Rothenstein, Director of the Graves Art Gallery.

This period also saw two changes in the Association's name. In 1930 the Derbyshire Council for the Preservation of the Countryside, under an agreement made nationally between the CPRE and rural community councils, changed its name to 'The CPRE Derbyshire County Committee'. Under this agreement it was proposed that various area committees formed by the county committee should also take the title 'CPRE' together with the name of their special local committee. In the light of this it was unanimously agreed to change the name of the Association to 'The Council for the Preservation of Rural England, Sheffield and Peak District Committee'. But it was minuted that it was to be understood that the newly named Committee would preserve its autonomy completely. The suggestion that the name Hallamshire instead of Sheffield might be more acceptable in Derbyshire was not pursued. Then in February 1934, the word Committee was dropped and Branch substituted. The Executive then became the Executive Committee. The new constitution of 1931 also meant that the organisation expanded numerically through the attraction of general members who supported the aims of the organisation, paid an annual subscription and received an annual report.

The six years from 1930 to the end of 1935 saw a continuation of the concerns and campaigns of the first six years, but with the increased professionalisation of the organisation and with the first stirrings of the two projects that would stand out above all others in its history: a green belt for Sheffield and the designation of the Peak District as a national park. There was also a sense that the organisation was entering a critical period. In the Annual Report for 1932 the point was strongly made that the powers for protecting the countryside were not keeping pace with the forces of destruction. The next few years were regarded as 'critical in the extreme'.

In April 1933 the Town and Country Planning Act came into force. Disappointing in some respects, it was seen by the Committee as a powerful instrument for safeguarding the countryside. The fact that only parts of the Peak District came under planning schemes was a continued cause of concern. As late as 1933 the Buxton, New Mills, Chapel-en-le-Frith and Hayfield areas, containing Kinder Scout and the watershed of the Wye, Dove and Dane, did not have a statutory planning scheme and neither had the area covered by Bakewell District Council including the villages of

Great and Little Longstone, Litton and Monyash, and the valleys of the Derwent and Wye.

II

Increased traffic in the 1930s meant that scenic routes and old river bridges continued to be under threat through road widening schemes. The proposal by the Ministry of Transport to widen the A6 road in the section between Derby and Buxton was the subject of debate in Executive meetings in 1930 and 1931. In October 1930 it was reported that the section of road from Cromford to Buxton had been walked and every detail likely to be affected by widening had been noted. The CPRE County Committee was to make a similar survey between Derby and Cromford, and on its completion, the two surveys were to be combined, and recommendations as to how the beauty of the road could be safeguarded would be submitted to the County Council. By February 1931 it was reported to the Executive by the Assistant

The Sheepwash Bridge, Ashford.

Secretary that the original road widening proposals had been considerably modified: expenditure had been lowered from an estimated £800,000 to £250,000 and the only places in the Committee's area that would be seriously affected would be at Taddington and Ashford, where by-passes were to be constructed. However, there was concern at Derbyshire County Council that Sheffield traffic would reach the by-pass at Ashford via the old sheepwash bridge which might have to be widened or a new bridge erected close by. The Executive made successful representations that the old bridge should be scheduled as an ancient monument to safeguard its future. There were also plans for drastic road widenings between Whirlow Bridge and Castleton in 1932 and detailed observations and objections were sent to Derbyshire County Council.

Increasing volumes of road traffic, commercial and private, also meant that the advertising industry continued to try to augment the existing number of advertisements along popular routes, not only within Derbyshire but within the rural parts of western Sheffield. But getting Sheffield to act decisively continued to be problematical. In February 1930 the Executive suggested to the Town Clerk that a conference should be organised to consider the question of advertisement regulation within the city boundary. A member of the Executive, Mr Samuel Osborn, had been made a member of the City Council's Improvement Committee, and he promised to use his influence in arranging a conference, but by October of 1930 nothing had been arranged. However, some progress had been made in other directions. The City Engineer had asked the Committee for suggestions for proposed bye-laws for petrol filling stations. These had been drawn up and sent to Sir Ernest Holderness at the Home Office. He considered them too severe, and revised recommendations, which were more likely to meet with the approval of the Home Office, were submitted to the City Engineer. They were eventually approved in 1934. The bye-laws not only controlled the design and siting of petrol stations within the city boundaries, but in certain specified areas, they prohibited them altogether. In 1935 the County Surveyor for the West Riding agreed to accept in large measure the Branch's recommendations about roadside advertising in those parts of the West Riding within the Peak District. This meant that advertisements were prohibited on the whole of the Strines road and parts of the Moscar, Langsett and Woodhead roads. Action by Derbyshire County Council in the northern part of the county meant that by 1932, pumps and oil boxes there had been painted green and advertisements in many cases removed.

The Sheffield City Engineer requested in 1930 that the Committee should re-submit their 1927 recommendations on advertising regulations in a different form. But it was not until September 1932 that the Secretary could report that Sheffield City Council had passed bye-laws controlling advertisements. These had been sent to the Home Office and had been strongly opposed by the British Advertising Company. Subsequently, most of their objections were withdrawn and the bye-laws were approved by the Home Office in 1933. In November 1934 it was reported that five members of the Branch had undertaken a survey of intrusive and inappropriate advertisements in Sheffield and a list of 60 advertisements which infringed the bye-laws had been sent to the City Surveyor who had expressed 'much gratitude'.

In Derbyshire where there were advertising bye-laws, there was continued concern that they were not always applied with the force that was appropriate. In October 1931 the Executive resolved to send a resolution to the Clerk of the County Council strongly supporting the Scapa Society which had promised to send evidence (including photographs) compiled by the Executive of unsightly advertisements in the county with the request that these should be removed. But success in Derbyshire continued to be limited. 'It is puzzling', it was stated in the 1933 Annual Report, 'that the Council, having made their bye-laws, seem unwilling to exercise them whole-heartedly'. However, when Sheffield's boundaries were extended further into Derbyshire in 1934, Sheffield City Council immediately took action against offending advertisements on the Owler Bar Road, on the road between Whirlow and Fox House, and in the Woodseats area.

Smoke pollution from Earle's Hope Valley Cement Works became an issue in 1930. Complaints had been received by the Derbyshire County Committee of the CPRE, but at a meeting between Mr Earle, the Secretary

Smoke from Earle's Hope Valley Cement Works.

of the County Committee, Ethel, and Phil Barnes, Earle had stated that the cost of reducing emissions was prohibitive and anyway the dust was not harmful to the surrounding land. At Phil Barnes' suggestion it was decided to conduct experiments but it was not found possible to arrange for these to be undertaken. Instead, evidence about the nuisance was sent to the Ministry of Health. The following year samples were collected from twelve experimental stations and analysed by Professor Fearnsides and his staff. By the end of 1931 it was reported that Earle's had installed dust separating apparatus and claimed that dust emissions had been reduced by 50 per cent and that they intended to reduce the level even further. Nevertheless, complaints were still being made by local residents. It was reported that there was no likelihood of the large volume of steam which was also emitted from the works, and which spoiled the rural aspect of the valley, being lowered to any appreciable extent.

Nothing intruding into the beauty of the Peak District escaped the attention of the Committee. As they raised their collective eyes upwards they were appalled to see that aviation had brought advertising-skywriting to the Peak District. A resolution was passed by the Executive in March 1932 pressing the Government to take immediate legislative action against it. The resolution was sent to all local MPs.

III

The issue of residential development, swallowing up the countryside and potentially built of inappropriate materials and in incongruous styles, occupied a great deal of the Executive Committee's time and that of specialist advisers. In the 1935 Annual Report, ribbon development and uncontrolled surburbanisation, in the absence of planning regulations, was reported to be causing considerable defacement in the High Peak:

> *This is noticeable in the Calver district, at Ashford, at Darley*
> *Dale, and especially in the Hope Valley. Bamford, Hope and*
> *Castleton are in danger of becoming mere collections of*
> *suburban villas and bungalows; the green upland between*
> *Shatton and Brough is advertised as a housing estate; while*
> *the once beautiful main road through the Hope valley is being*
> *rapidly sacrificed to disorder and ribbon development.*

The report went on to point out that nearer Sheffield there was no security for the beautiful approaches at Ringinglow, Dore Moor, Redmires, Hollow

Ribbon development in incongruous designs and inappropriate building materials.

Meadows, the Owler Bar road and the Porter Valley. Crosspool, Crimicar and Ecclesall were fast succumbing to 'scarlet fever' and 'the once dignified stone village of Dore' had become 'the stage of pseudo-Tudor'.

In 1930 a special Peak District Advisory Panel of Architects was set up by the Committee, consisting of members nominated by the Sheffield, South Yorkshire and District Society of Architects and Surveyors, the Nottingham, Derby and Lincoln Architectural Society, and approved by the RIBA and the Ministry of Health. The Committee also decided to publish a pamphlet giving advice on building design and building materials. Sixteen hundred copies were sent to builders, contractors, estate agents, landowners and local authorities. The pamphlet made it clear what the Panel was and what its role was intended to be. It was pointed out that members of the Panel would be glad to examine, free of charge, any plans submitted to them, and make suggestions about design, choice of materials and surroundings. It was made clear that the Panel did not take a dictatorial position, but would offer suitable architectural advice to further the aims of the CPRE.

The main emphasis of the pamphlet was that the Peak District was 'stone country' and the farms and villages were built in stone in a plain traditional style 'in perfect harmony with the landscape' and increased its beauty. The increasing use of unsuitable colours and materials was deprecated although it was acknowledged that it was now usually impossible to build entirely of stone. Modern materials, it was pointed out, were not necessarily unsuitable and the use of 'stone coloured' materials was an inexpensive alternative. The fashion for 'half-timber work' was also frowned upon.

The case work of the Panel, described in the 1934 Annual Report as 'the most vital and difficult of the Committee's activities', increased over the next two years and in 1932 its area was enlarged to include north-east Derbyshire. In the latter area, a large proportion of the cases originated with the surveyor there, who was reported to be 'sparing no effort to preserve the character of the region'. Among many cases dealt with between 1930–35 were a Forestry Commission bungalow near the Snake Inn, where three earlier bungalows had been in red brick and purple slate; a scheme for forty cottages for workers at Hope Cement Works; a group of eight houses at Dungworth by Wortley Rural District Council, who had been persuaded to use stone-coloured brick; a scheme for 80 houses for Bakewell Rural District Council; and a fire station designed by the Panel for the main street at Hathersage at the request of the Parish Council.

It was a matter of reasoning with and persuading private individuals, builders and local authority representatives. Sometimes the Panel succeeded, sometimes it failed, as described in the 1933 Annual Report:

> *Three examples will serve as illustrations. A timber bungalow with red-asbestos roof, proposed to be erected in a stone hamlet, was changed to one with Cotswold-grey tiles and stone-coloured stucco walls. Bad designs for villas in a conspicuous position on the outskirts of an old village were completely redrawn to harmonise in form and colour with the surroundings. The builder of a new estate in an unspoilt rural district of Sheffield was interviewed in the hope that he could be persuaded to refrain from using red pressed bricks entirely out of keeping with the surroundings; but, unfortunately, he expressed himself unable to acquiesce in the Panel's recommendations, at least in regard to the majority of houses.*

In order to influence architects, builders and developers, the Committee, through its Secretaries, sought to increase the availability of modern alternatives to local stone. The local agent of Asbestos Cement Building Products Ltd informed the Secretary in late 1932 that, owing to the influence of the Committee, his firm was finding it more difficult to sell pink and red asbestos roofing, and had brought some new 'mingled' brown, buff and green asbestos tiles for the Committee's opinion. In 1933 it was reported that all local brick manufacturers had been asked if they could produce a cheap stone-coloured brick, and the Sheffield Brick Company had succeeded in doing so.

There was also concern over the lack of control of building elevations in the rural areas within Sheffield's boundaries and it was not until 1933 that the bye-laws to control elevations were put into force. The City Surveyor asked if, unofficially, he could have the advice of the Panel. But this arrangement was not well received by members of the Highways Committee. It was reported at an Executive meeting in July 1933 that the Assistant Secretary had been to the Town Hall every fortnight over the previous four months to assist the City Surveyor on building elevation matters, had subsequently visited sites that might cause bad disfigurement and had submitted written recommendations. However, members of the Highways Committee had expressed resentment of his recommendations over a recent case, and the Chairman had expressed the view that it was illegal for an outside body to see plans, and that the fortnightly visits should be discontinued. The Executive was then reduced to sending petitions to the Town Clerk about building elevation issues, until the composition of the Highways Committee was changed, when more sympathetic members were to be approached.

A significant development in influencing, builders, developers and local authorities about building design, location and materials, took place in April 1934 with the publication of the booklet *Housing in the Peak District*. Covering 72 pages, it had been compiled and illustrated by the Assistant Secretary, John Worsnip, and contained a large number of photographs including a number of outstanding ones by Phil Barnes, and constituted a comprehensive guide to building in the Peak District. In his hard-hitting Foreword, Guy Dawber, a Past President of the Royal Institute of British Architects, went straight into the attack:

> *The beauty of our English countryside is daily disfigured, not only by the thoughtlessness of speculative builders, but also through the apathy and indifference of the public, for there are today great numbers of people, many in responsible positions, who think that the present has no obligations either to the past or to the future, and that if a man wants to build a house he need consider only his own convenience or profit, and that it may be as ugly and out of place as he chooses to make it.*

He went on

> *The problem of saving the countryside cannot be solved by legislation—it is a matter of goodwill on the part of the public. Had we taught, fifty years ago, the people of this country, adults and children in our elementary, secondary and public schools and universities, the value of our beautiful countryside its trees and scenery, its villages, churches and old buildings, and objects of historic interest—civic pride in fact—we should not to-day be suffering from this spate of ugliness that is overwhelming the whole country.*

By the end of July over 2000 copies of the booklet had been disposed of. Every effort was made to get the booklet into the hands of the local authorities and to this end a copy was sent to every clerk and surveyor in the Peak District and surrounding areas. Seventy copies were sent to reviewers, and reviews appeared in the popular press and professional and technical journals. Interesting orders included 30 copies for Ashbourne Rural District Council, where matters were obviously taken very seriously, and 44 for Leeds School of Architecture. In March 1935 it was reported that 31 copies had been ordered for the Lake District Panel, and that the publication of the booklet was encouraging the idea of similar publications for Cheshire, Cornwall and the Lake District. Requests for copies had also been received from as far away as New York and Montreal. But it was not received at first with approval from every quarter. The Sheffield & District House Builders' Association had been annoyed at its publication and had even threatened legal action. They then wrote to the Branch asking if the CPRE could offer any *constructive* recommendations and asking for representation on the Panel.

Housing in the Peak District was followed in 1935 by a portfolio of drawings of inexpensive houses and bungalows appropriate in design and use of materials to the Peak District. The thirteen designs had been chosen by means of a competition judged by a distinguished panel of judges— Professor Patrick Abercrombie, Guy Dawber and Hubert Worthington, the Manchester architect. They were devised for use by builders, local authorities and individuals not in a position to employ an architect, on payment of a fee of £2 per house to the Panel. In 1936 the designs were made available in abbreviated form in an attractive booklet, *Small Houses and Bungalows suitable for the Peak District*. A permanent exhibition of suitable building materials was displayed at Endcliffe Vale House to coincide with the publication of *Housing in the Peak District*.

A DETACHED HOUSE

ALTERNATIVE MATERIALS:
STUCCO
STONE COLOURED BRICKS
STONE

APPROXIMATE COST
£490————£540

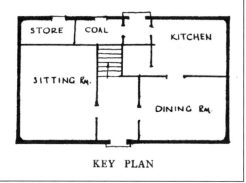

KEY PLAN

An illustration from Small Houses and Bungalows suitable for the Peak District *(1936),*
which showed in simplified form the house designs available from the Branch from 1935.

IV

On two other fronts the Committee met only with mixed success. There was the ever-present possibility of the building of reservoirs, thus changing the character of large areas through the flooding of valleys, loss of amenity and the possible planting of large blocks of conifers around reservoirs. The Stockport scheme for the Goyt Valley, which had first appeared on the agenda in 1929, continued to be a focus of concern in 1930 and 1931, even though it lay beyond the boundaries of the Committee's concern. It was reported at the June 1930 meeting of the Executive that the Bill had been approved by a Select Committee of the House of Commons. Owing to considerable opposition to the scheme, footpaths had been protected and a clause to safeguard the surroundings of the reservoirs inserted. But the CPRE in London let it be known that it was disappointed that stronger precautions had not been taken to protect amenity interests and it was decided to send a joint memorandum to Stockport Corporation on behalf of the Derbyshire County Committee of the CPRE, the Sheffield and Peak District Committee, the Manchester Ramblers' Federation and the Peak District Footpaths Society. The memorandum was drawn up by Phil Barnes. By early 1934 concern was concentrated on the proposed new reservoir at Ladybower in the Derwent valley and the submerging of the river scenery from Derwent Village to Yorkshire Bridge, of Derwent Hall and the Packhorse Bridge. Tenants had received notice to quit but little specific information was available. The Committee found itself to be powerless except to make representations about building materials and tree planting.

The Committee also continued to battle with electricity companies about the impact on the Peak District scenery of overhead wires and supports. In 1930, together with the Secretary of the Derbyshire County Committee, Phil Barnes had suggested an alternative and less disfiguring route for the line between Chinley and Hayfield, but it proved impossible to obtain the necessary way leaves. Prolonged efforts to save the river walk between Hathersage and Shatton from overhead cables were unsuccessful, with only a short section of the line being buried underground. Supply lines were also multiplying in the Hope Valley where the Yorkshire Electric Power Company, which supplied the Hope Cement Works, proposed to extend supplies to the villages of Bamford, Hope and Castleton. In the event, after a Ministry Inquiry at Hope, some accommodation was achieved and the company agreed to bury the low tension mains underground throughout the centre of Castleton, the centre of Bamford, and near the church at Hope. Cables were also placed underground in the Peak Cavern Gorge. Some success was also achieved at Foolow and Litton in 1932 where the Derby & Notts Power Company agreed to erect their lines behind rather than in front of the houses and at Litton to bury the line across the village green. At Barlow, the line through the village was only taken underground when a private gift of £20 was offered to ease the situation!

V

Amidst the ceaseless campaigning and lobbying on specific fronts, the Committee realised that it must continue the task of educating public opinion and gaining the sympathy and active support of town and country dwellers alike. This was dealt with at Executive meetings under what today seems the rather sinister heading of 'Propaganda'. The 1929 'Save the Countryside' Exhibition continued to tour outlying parts of the Committee's area and beyond in the early 1930s, and Ethel and Phil Barnes also spread the message through 'lantern talks' ('a telling method of propaganda') to audiences large and small throughout the Peak District and beyond. Early 1930 also saw the first intimation that a book might be prepared, chiefly consisting of photographs dealing with, in Ethel's words, 'the various kinds of disfigurement in relation to scenery' and by June it was reported that the work of taking photographs for the book was under way. It was published in December 1931 as *The Threat to the Peak*.

Seventy years on, *The Threat to the Peak* is still a very powerful document. Of large format, and elegant design, it is written in a direct style, expertly edited by Ethel, and beautifully illustrated with black and white photographs, mainly by Phil Barnes, and drawings of flowers by H.H. Peach. Its impact on the general public, local government officers and politicians and members of the rambling fraternity can only be imagined. Its message is clear and compelling and the tone is set right at the outset in the Foreword by Professor G.M. Trevelyan:

> *...Much of the Peak District, as of all other beautiful districts, will doubtless be more or less spoiled, but much may yet be saved—not by a single process, but by a combination of methods of action and restraint, increasingly applied by individuals and by the community. This little book is a word of counsel and exhortation, a 'humble petition and advice' to the inhabitants, visitors, owners and public bodies in whose hands the fate of the Peak District lies.*
>
> *The tide of public opinion is moving with great rapidity in the direction of a new demand for the preservation of natural*

Derwent Edge, one of Phil Barnes' photographs used in the Threat to the Peak *(1931).*

Another Phil Barnes photograph from The Threat to the Peak *illustrating the impact of garish advertising at petrol stations. The caption is 'Is this fair to Bakewell?'*

beauty. The young, on the average, feel it more keenly than the old. Outrages cheerfully perpetrated twenty years ago 'and nothing said,' would be impossible to-day. Outrages possible to-day will be impossible twenty years hence. The future is on our side in no small degree, if we can hold the fort for another generation. And in the realm of educating opinion, it is such work as this which the CPRE is doing in which the hope for the future lies.

There follows a preface in the form of a word picture of the changing landscapes of the Peak from south to north accompanied by page after page—fourteen in all—of stunning photographs of Peakland scenery at all seasons as seen through Phil Barnes's camera and educated eye. There are then eleven short chapters that drive home the conservation message: on building style and building materials (with particularly harsh words about Sheffield, saying of the 'uncontrolled vulgarity' of the western suburbs: 'One is shamed as a citizen to look on this despoliation'); on intrusive advertising; on litter; on the preservation of wildlife; on the proliferation of petrol-filling stations; about road building and ribbon development; about beautiful and ugly bridges; about electricity trans-mission lines and pylons; about uncontrolled tipping; and about industry in the countryside. All the chapters are accompanied by telling photographs which show the good, the bad and the downright ugly and all crisply captioned: 'Matlock as God made it'…AND as improved by man (ugly bridges and garish advertising); 'A bridge of little charm'; 'Is this fair to Bakewell?' (a petrol station covered in strident advertising). The book ends with an epilogue: 'The Necessity of Town and Country Planning'.

By the end of 1933, 3,300 copies had been disposed of including, on publication, complimentary copies to every member of the Standing Com-mittee of the House of Commons dealing with the Town and Country Planning Bill, and to the Prime Minister, Ramsey Macdonald, and to the Prince of Wales.

It was received with acclamation by almost all sections of the popular press and by professional journals, attracting about 40 reviews in all. Reviewers commented on the beauty of the book itself as well as the values it espoused. *The Times* said it was 'both beautiful in itself and should bring new beauty to the country whence it hails'. In similar vein the *Manchester Guardian* commented that the photographs were the 'best pictures of Peak country that we have seen…an inspiring manual of defensive tactics'. In a book review in the *Manchester Guardian*, in February 1932, Ivor Brown was moved to write that 'Even with the February wind howling about the house, the pictures sing a beckoning song'. The *Daily Sketch* said it was

'A beautiful book which is at one and the same time saddening and heartening' and in the view of the *News Chronicle* it was 'an eloquent plea, splendidly printed and illustrated'. The local press was also fulsome in its praise. The *Sheffield Daily Telegraph* concluded that it was 'A remarkable volume…We hope this book will be widely read…Few local publications have possessed so much real importance.' The *Sheffield Independent* said it was an 'appeal which should touch the sympathies of all people who know the Derbyshire countryside'. Among the professional journals the *Architects' Journal* said 'How well the CPRE have carried out their job' and the *Municipal Journal* said it was 'A timely warning'. Even *The Builder*, many of whose readers must have been outraged by the book or what they read about it in the press, said 'Here is a telling indictment of the carelessness and folly which have characterised the growth of our modern towns'.

The only sour note was engendered by coverage in the *Daily Express*. In what Phil Barnes promptly called a 'garbled' review in letters to the press, the writer in that newspaper interpreted the book as an attack solely on Sheffield Corporation. The Town Hall must have been inundated by telephone calls, and officials and councillors must have been 'incandescent'. In a report in the *Manchester Daily Dispatch*, W.J. Hadfield, the City Surveyor, justified the Council's non-intervention in controlling the style of housing in the rural parts of the city, saying the City Council 'could not stop people expressing their individuality in building. The Corporation cannot dictate on matters of taste'. More intemperately, in a report in the *Daily Express*, he went further and impugned the Committee, being quoted as saying, condescendingly, that it was made up of 'well-meaning people' and that 'cranks are always to be found in any organisation'.

VI

Another outstanding achievement, on a par with the Longshaw purchase, was the resolution of the Blacka Moor issue through the purchase of the property in 1933 by the benefactor, Alderman J.G. Graves, and its presentation to the City of Sheffield as an open space for public enjoyment in perpetuity.

Ethel later recalled the circumstances in which Alderman Graves bought Blacka Moor. Norton Rural District Council, had 'held the fort' since 1929 by adopting a draft Town Planning Scheme and refusing all facilities for building. But it could not go on resisting for ever and it was in no position to pay the compensation that would have been necessary if permission to develop the area was finally refused:

We were doubtful about the results of an Enquiry and the Norton Council was poor. There was the last hope of Sheffielders—Alderman Graves. The late Mr. F.W. Scorah approached the Alderman and I supplemented the attack. He scarcely knew Blacka at the time and seemed rather indifferent. I begged him just to go through the wood which hides the view from the main road. We learnt afterwards that on doing so, he cast his eyes over the sweep of the Blacka hills, and said within himself 'It's mine'.

A few days later I received a momentous telephone call. It was Mr Scorah, who said in a quiet voice, 'Graves thinks he will'. And, as you know, Graves did.

Ethel further recalled standing with Alderman Graves after the public opening of Blacka Moor.

'Now, after we've done all this for you (by 'we' he meant the Graves Trust) will you promise never to trouble us again?'

I took a deep breath, thought I'd better be truthful and said, 'Whenever the countryside around Sheffield is in danger, I shall appeal to you'. He looked at me, severely but not unkindly. 'Well' he said, 'now we know'.

The ceremony at Blacka Moor in 1933 when the area was handed over to the City of Sheffield by Alderman Graves.

VII

The six year period from 1930 to 1935 was a momentous one. The bank overdraft on Longshaw was paid off and the property handed over to the National Trust in 1931, Blacka Moor was saved from development in 1933, the Advisory Panel of Architects began to have a major impact on building design and use of appropriate materials, influence had been successfully exerted on a wide range of issues as diverse as advertising bye-laws and the routing and burying of electricity transmission lines, and through its publications and other promotional activities, the voice of the Branch (as it had become in 1934) was being heard and its mission understood in more and more places and by more and more people. With the change of constitution in 1931, membership had risen from the original twelve in 1924 to nearly 500 by the end of 1935.

The purchase of land in the Porter Valley by the Graves Trust in 1932, the subsequent purchase by the same body of Blacka Moor in 1933, and the forestalling of housing development on a 14-acre site on the Owler Bar road at Totley foreshadowed the Branch's aspiration that a more comprehensive scheme could be devised to protect the rural western parts of Sheffield. It was also during this period that the idea of a national park in the Peak District was first discussed. This was the result of a proposal submitted to the National Parks Committee in 1930 by the Joint Ramblers' Federations, supported by Manchester City Council and the Regional Town-Planning Committee in North West England, to create a national park in the High Peak (including Dovedale).

A green belt for Sheffield and a national park in the Peak District were to be major concerns for the Branch during the rest of the 1930s.

3

Mapping the future
1936–1939

I

WITH THE DEPARTURE OF JOHN WORSNIP in October 1935, the search was on for his immediate replacement and advertisements were placed in *The Times*, *The Architects' Journal* and *The Architect & Building News* during November. Gerald Haythornthwaite, recently qualified in architecture at Manchester University, and employed since June as an assistant architect by Thomas Worthington and Sons, Architects, of Manchester, was shown the advertisement by Professor Cordingley of the School of Architecture at Manchester University to whom he had gone to request a reference for another post for which he intended to apply.

Gerald wrote to Ethel Gallimore on 19 November 1935 expressing an interest in the post and asking if it were too late to send an application. Ethel replied positively on 21 November and included a number of CPRE booklets. His formal letter of application, dated 23 November, was admirably succinct:

> *I wish to apply for the post of Assistant Secretary to the Sheffield and Peak District branch of the C.P.R.E.*
>
> *I am well aware of the nature of the work entailed and am deeply interested in it. If one has other than commercial interests in Architecture a national organisation such as the C.P.R.E. offers more scope and opportunity for self-expression than private practice, therefore I welcome the chance to be active in this direction.*
>
> *I have completed my courses at the University for exemption from the R.I.B.A. final examination and hold the University*

> *Diploma in Architecture. During these courses I won both the Senior and Junior Design Prizes of the Manchester Society of Architects. I have studied Town Planning for a period of two years at the University and I adopted a Town Planning subject for my Final Design Thesis. It is my intention to continue these studies with a view to taking the Institute of Town Planners examination.*

Interestingly, someone, presumably Ethel, underlined in pencil the phrases 'Senior and Junior Design Prizes' and 'taking the Institute of Town Planners examination'.

On 25 November Ethel wrote to Gerald inviting him to come for interview, which took place before the end of the month. In the light of what was to happen subsequently, it is interesting that Ethel followed up the letter of 25 November with another one asking two questions:

> *One is, will you tell me your age please? The other, if you took this place and got on satisfactorily, would you be prepared to stay not less than two or three years? I ask this, because there is so much about the locality and the people we deal with to learn, that it takes some months to get into the job. It would be a bad thing for our work here if the Asst. Sec. were changed often. The last two each stayed three years.*

In the event Gerald stayed for the rest of his life—59 years!

Gerald's application was accompanied by an open testimonial from Hubert Worthington, one of the principals at Thomas Worthington and Sons. Two references were also received following the interview, one from his old Professor, Reginald Cordingley, and the other again from Hubert Worthington. Worthington's testimonial was positive:

> *Mr Haythornthwaite, who has been in our office about six months, tells me that he is applying for the Assistant Secretaryship of the Sheffield & Peak Branch of the C.P.R.E. He came to us from the Manchester University School of Architecture after taking the five year course and qualifying as A.R.I.B.A. We do not want to lose him, as he is keen and becoming increasingly useful, but he says he has got a 'vocation' for C.P.R.E. work which is important, and that he would rather do that type of work than be in practice. He is keen on the country and on rock climbing.*

> *I cannot speak from personal knowledge of his literary or oratorical capacity, but he tells me that he edited the Architecture School paper and had thought of trying to get on the staff of an architectural paper. He has done a lot of speaking at the University Union on general subjects and on architecture at students' meetings.*
>
> *He is a good draughtsman and no doubt would develop on the special lines that the C.P.R.E. would require.*
>
> *Obviously you will want to see him and catechise him on his points of view, but he is keen and energetic, and would probably make a very useful man for the job.*

Worthington's confidential reference on the other hand was rather muted and dwelt on Gerald's shortcomings.

> *I cannot tell you very much about Haythornthwaite because he has only been with us six months, and I did not know him before. He of course has yet to prove himself, and his lettering is not first rate, and I gather he has not done very much freehand sketching of really domestic buildings, etc. When he first told me that he was applying for the job I asked him about this, and told him that if he got it he would have to make himself master of that type of thing, as it would be essential for you. He has not been working on rural buildings for us, but I imagine that he has an appreciation of local style and materials, but of course he has had, presumably, a very complete education which should enable him to build up experience and develop on special lines if he is appointed.*

Professor Cordingley's was more fulsome. After explaining the circumstances in which he drew Gerald's attention to the advertisement, he continued

> *He has some leanings towards literary work in the field of architecture and, I think, feels that the appointment would allow him scope in such connection, without severing him from practical professional experience.*
>
> *The position appears to fit his capacity admirably. He is fully qualified as an architect, except that he has yet a few months of practical experience to complete before he becomes eligible for Associateship of the Royal Institute of British Architects. This requirement is a formal one, he having completed all his examination requirements. He is already eligible to be entered on the (Parliamentary) Register of Architects.*

There then followed another paragraph about his trustworthiness and family background and then Cordingley concluded by saying 'I am glad you have interviewed him. He is well liked here, and I am sure you would always find him obliging and helpful.'

Gerald was offered the post on 4 December and reported for work immediately after the New Year on 2 January 1936. The letter of appointment from Ethel contained one sentence that probably dampened his delight at securing the post: 'I might say that the standard of lettering and draughtsmanship as shown in the drawings you left here is not quite up to our previous standard…'

So the young tyro, with only six months' professional experience, and with no local knowledge of people or places, was thrown in at the deep end.

In less than eighteen months, because his relationship with Ethel had become a romantic one, Gerald beat a diplomatic retreat: he resigned and took up a post in the City Architect's Department at Sheffield City Council, but continued to work unofficially in close collaboration with Ethel. They married in December 1937 and honeymooned in Swaledale.

Gerald's place as Assistant Secretary was taken by Stanley Meyrick, a Liverpool trained architect. Meyrick stayed until March 1939 when he took up a post under the County Architect of Derbyshire County Council. At that point Gerald, who had been invited onto the Executive Committee the previous December, was re-appointed, this time as Technical Secretary. He held this position for only a few months before being called up with his Territorial unit at the outbreak of hostilities in September.

II

The first substantive item on the agenda of the first Executive Committee meeting in 1936 was what was called 'Preservation of Rural Areas in Sheffield forming Approaches to the Moors'. It contained the good news that Sheffield Highways Committee had proposed that under the Restriction of Ribbon Development Act (1935), not only the main roads but also over 200 unclassified roads in the rural parts of the city should be scheduled. This had been approved by the City Council without objection. In April 1936 the Ministry of Health approved the scheduling of 80 unclassified roads within the City boundary. This did not necessarily mean that the City Council would apply the Act in the case of these roads, but it had the powers to do so.

The bad news was that a speculative builder had purchased 84 acres on the north side of Hathersage Road between Whirlow Bridge and Long Line and an adjacent field of nine acres on the south side of the road opposite the Dore Moor Inn, and intended to build 900 houses on the two sites. Local residents had been encouraged by Ethel to mount a campaign, including letters to the press, and a promise to raise the necessary compensation if necessary, and the City Council had been made aware that there was considerable opposition against the proposal.

Ethel recalled 40 years later, during an address to mark the 50th birthday of the CPRE, going to see Alderman Fred Marshall about the matter.

> *I said I knew we could not save <u>all</u> the rural areas adjoining Sheffield, but I did hope we could save some of the specially favourite ones; such as Lodge Moor to Stanage or Whirlow to Dore Moor. He looked at me very steadfastly and said, 'We must <u>save it all</u>'. I shall never forget how my heart leapt at these words; at the realisation we might have official backing for our ideals.*

Alderman Fred Marshall, MP.

In February 1936 a deputation from the Branch consisting of Ethel, Professor Forster, the Hon. Francis Balfour (representing Lord Riverdale), Mr A.C. Davy (representing Whirlow and Dore residents), Dr C.D. Holdsworth and Mr Samuel Osborn, went to the Town Hall to put its case before the Highways Committee. The 1936 Annual Report stated that besides putting their objections to the Whirlow case, they took the opportunity to state that the time had come to 'fix some limit as to where the town should end and the country begin', and that suburbs should not be allowed to spread right up to the edge of the moors. They reminded the committee that the official Civic Survey conducted by Professor Abercrombie had reserved the area for public open spaces or sports grounds. Finally, it was suggested that the moment was opportune to consider 'the securing of a permanent Green Belt, comprising the hill country west of the city'. Thirteen other societies also organised petitions to the City Council.

Largely due to the influence of Alderman Marshall, the Highways Committee rejected the proposed Whirlow development and paid the large sum of £22,000 in compensation to the builder. The Whirlow campaign caused the idea of a green belt to take hold in the minds of members of the public and there was pressure to secure such a barrier to wholesale development on all sides of the city where farmland and woods had survived. Again Alderman Marshall was instrumental in moving the idea forward. At the Executive Meeting in September 1936 he stated that he was taking a great personal interest in securing the green belt on all sides of the city. He considered the first action of the newly formed Planning Committee should be to decide which areas were to remain rural and which should be built on.

Later that autumn the Branch was officially invited by the Town Planning Advisory Committee to submit proposals in the form of a map 'as to areas on all sides of Sheffield which might suitably be preserved as a Green or Agricultural Belt'. The deadline was the middle of January 1937. The survey was carried out by Ethel and Gerald. The map and recommendations were submitted on 1 February and came before the Planning Committee on 12 April. The recommendations fell under five headings.

The first identified those areas that should be preserved as a green belt. The largest area was the area of moorland and upland pasture dotted with 'stone farms' whose development, it was stated, would not only inflict on the citizens of Sheffield an irreparable loss but would also 'injure the city's prestige'. This area comprised large parts of the Dore and Totley area, Ringinglow, Redmires and Stanage, the Porter and Rivelin valleys, Wyming Brook, Blacka Moor, and Burbage and Houndkirk Moors. In the north-west Birley Edge and Beeley Wood were identified as worthy of inclusion in the green belt. In the south, strips of farmland, at Totley, Norton and Hemsworth,

Looking towards Upper Hurst Farm from Back Edge, part of Sheffield's provisional Green Belt to the north-west of the continuously built-up area.

lying adjacent to large areas of agricultural land in Derbyshire, were recommended for inclusion. In the east and north-east 'largely disfigured through industrial development', Ballifield Green and the Shirtcliff Valley, Woolley Wood, Tinsley Golf Course and High Hazels Park were included.

The second set of recommendations dealt with how areas included within the green belt should be treated. They should be kept 'strictly rural', was the recommendation, with no building allowed except for agricultural purposes. The proximity of working farmland meant a near and fresh food supply to Sheffield and prevented the city's residents from being 'unhealthily divorced from country conditions'. Another good use for green belt land in some areas would be for playing fields.

The third set of recommendations dealt with the important issue of co-operating with adjacent local authorities. Sheffield was much smaller in extent than it is today, and areas to the north were still part of West Riding County Council under Wortley Rural District Council, places such as Stannington, Bradfield, the upper part of the Loxley valley, and Ecclesfield parish including the rural areas around Grenoside. To the south co-operation was necessary with the various planning authorities within Derbyshire, especially the Chesterfield Regional Planning Committee, to protect the area bounded by Dronfield Woodhouse, Coal Aston, Mosbrough and Eckington, including the particularly attractive countryside around Troway and Ford.

The fourth set of recommendations dealt with the control of the appearance of buildings. New buildings should be few and far between. Where new building was necessary or alterations were proposed, they should be of local stone including the roofs. In exceptional circumstances less expensive, stone-coloured materials might be used. The advice of the joint CPRE/RIBA Advisory Panel of Architects was recommended.

Finally the Planning Committee was reminded of the various means of securing land for inclusion in the green belt: purchase by the Corporation from its own resources or by public appeal, scheduling as 'private open space', and private gift.

Green belt proposals by the Planning Committee, based largely on the recommendations of the Branch, were eventually approved the City Council on 1 June 1938. Areas in the Handsworth and Norton areas and in the north-west of the City had been excluded. The proposals had been approved only by a small majority, and the whole of the Progressive Party had voted against. In view of this opposition the Branch deemed it was necessary to watch carefully for all attempts to encroach upon the green belt.

In the period between being asked to submit green belt recommendations and their approval by the City Council, there were some welcome developments in the form of purchases by the City Council of land in the proposed green belt: 70 acres of land, including farms, south of Forge Dam in the Porter Valley; land in Mickley Lane, Totley, where building was threatened; land in Limestone Cottage Lane at Wadsley where building was proposed; and Norton Grange and eight acres of land. On the other hand, the euphoria surrounding the City Council's decision to approve the green belt was severely quashed by the loss of land to building at Gleadless within the approved belt, believed to be the result of a difference of opinion between the planning officers for Sheffield and Chesterfield Rural District Council (in whose jurisdiction it turned out to be). Sheffield City Council made some amends by deciding to buy Hazlebarrow Farm and 250 acres of land as a 'permanent agricultural reservation'. But another setback came in the form of the compulsory acquisition by the Air Ministry in early 1939 of land between Lightwood and Gleadless for a Balloon Barrage. The

Ministry had been offered a site at Tinsley but had refused it because of
subsidence. By March 1939, the former farmland was being prepared for
huts to accommodate 400 men. Treatment of buildings in green belt land
was also causing concern. Farm buildings at Blacka Moor and Dore Moor
had been repaired and extended with unsuitable materials.

It was clear by the outbreak of war in 1939 that the identification of a
green belt for Sheffield and its approval by the City Council, was only the
beginning. Approval of the provisional green belt was the first campaign
in a long war of attrition, a war that would last for more than four decades.

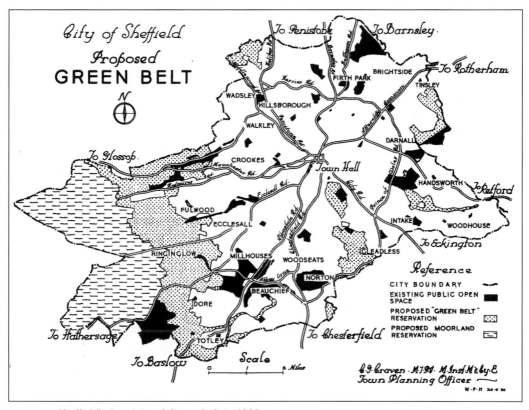

Sheffield's Provisional Green Belt in 1938.

III

Following close on the heels of the work on compiling a green belt map
and set of recommendations, another 'Save the Countryside' exhibition

A feature on the 1937 'Save the Countryside' Exhibition in the Sheffield Telegraph *published on 15 November 1937. The photographs, under the banner headline 'A CAMERA-INTERVIEW ON THE FIGHT FOR THE COUNTRY', show Ethel (1) enrolling new members, (2) emphasising the need for vigilance in protecting Sheffield's Green Belt, (3) showing 'stone-coloured' building materials in keeping with local character, and (4) explaining the features of the Longshaw estate.*

was held, building on the experience of 1929. It took place at the Graves Art Gallery whose Director, Dr John Rothenstein, it will be remembered, was a member of the Executive Committee. The exhibition was held over a three week period from 6 to 26 November 1937 and attracted 16,385 visitors.

The opening ceremony was held in the lecture theatre in the Central Library. The Branch chairman, Professor Forster, presided, the mayor-elect, Councillor E.G. Rowlinson, declared the exhibition open, and Sir William Rothenstein, the new President of the Branch, was the main speaker. Sir William spoke of the apathy of the British public about 'the cancer of destruction that was eating into its beauty'. More controversially he said he was afraid that much of the building currently taking place was 'but to ensure the provision of slums a hundred years hence'. He said that after inspecting the exhibition he could not imagine a clearer or more eloquent statement of the aims of the CPRE or a better way of appealing to the public. Among the dignitaries present at the opening ceremony were Alderman Graves; Alderman Marshall; the Chairman of Staffordshire County Council; the Vice-Chairman of Derbyshire County Council; and the Clerk of the Derwent Valley Water Board.

The exhibition itself consisted, as had become the hallmark of all the Branch's 'propaganda', of a series of large and striking photographs, beautifully presented on the walls of the gallery on green cards with white frames with white-lettered captions done by two ex-Sheffield College of Arts students. The photographs included a substantial number by Phil Barnes and others by Brian Blakemore, Paul Crimp, Tom Wing, Gerald Haythornthwaite, and the photographers of the *Sheffield Telegraph* and *Daily Independent*. The visitor was first confronted with sepia-toned photographs of beautiful Peak District scenery and villages and farms in harmony with scenery. Then came a series of cards on modern building form and material, contrasting those in traditional style built of stone with 'horrors' built in vulgar and ornate styles in highly coloured bricks and tiles. Other sections of the exhibition mounted round the walls dealt with the work of the Advisory Panel of Architects, the proposed Sheffield Green Belt, endangered beauty spots, and disfigurement by industry, electricity supply, ribbon development, and tipping and litter. Other displays were provided by the Peak Joint Planning Committee, Sheffield Town Planning Department, Derbyshire Architect's Department, and Chesterfield Regional Planning Committee. *The Manchester Guardian's* special correspondent commented on the clever captioning of the photographs in the disfigurement section 'some soberly expository, some humorous, and some bitterly

Dovedale. (Phil Barnes)

caustic—and even more effectively driven home by the exemplary simplicity and good taste which characterise every detail in the lay-out of the exhibition.' His comments on the green belt exhibit were equally eye-catching: 'a somewhat disconnected girdle, sadly belated and still largely unrealised...'. The centre of the gallery contained a display of building materials suitable for use in the Peak District and by models of the viaduct and workers' housing at the Ladybower Reservoir.

The exhibition caught the attention not only of the local and regional press, where detailed reports of the exhibits and Sir William Rothenstein's speech appeared and a lively correspondence ensued, but was also widely reported in the national press with substantial reports in *The Times*, the *Manchester Guardian* and the *Daily Herald*. The popular press and local newspapers in other regions as far away as Greenock and Sidmouth only reported Sir William Rothenstein's comments that many suburban houses would not last 100 years and that slums were being built on the edges of cities. On the day after the opening ceremony Sir William broadcast on the BBC Northern Programme from a studio in the Grand Hotel in Sheffield (Ethel had suggested this to the BBC before asking Sir William!). His title was 'The Northern Scene' and he linked his talk directly to the 'Save the Countryside' exhibition and the need for what he called 'a decently planned country'. In such a country 'the orderless agglomeration of small villa residences which now choke up the suburbs' would be replaced by 'measures to plan and build in a seemly manner' and town dwellers would have ready access to 'an unviolated countryside'. He concluded his talk by warmly congratulating the Branch's 'energetic and resourceful secretary' and hoped that similar enterprise would be shown in other parts of the country. His talk was published in *The Listener* on 24 November 1937.

The exhibition subsequently went on tour, and over the next three years appeared in whole or part in Bakewell, Burton, Buxton, Chesterfield, Derby, Hanley, Mansfield, Rotherham and Stafford.

IV

At the Executive Meeting of the Branch in August 1937 it was reported that a deputation from the Standing Committee on National Parks to the Parliamentary Secretary to the Minister of Health, urging that immediate steps be taken to set up a National Parks Commission as recommended in the 1931 Report of the Government Committee on National Parks, 'failed to secure a practical result'. As a consequence of this, and in view of the very wide public support for national parks, of which neither the Government nor the Ministry of Health were 'yet fully aware', CPRE headquarters had drafted a resolution to the Ministry of Health and asked every branch to send it to the Ministry. This action was unanimously approved and in addition the Branch resolved that, after the autumn exhibition was over, a sub-committee would be formed to act on Professor Abercrombie's suggestion at the Annual Meeting held in May 1937 that the Branch should map out areas in the Peak District suitable to include in a National Park.

The first meeting of the sub-committee was postponed on a number of occasions while background information was gathered and analysed, including the precise details of the proposal for a national park in the Peak District presented to the National Park Committee (Addison Committee) by the Manchester Ramblers' Federation in 1930. This proposal had suggested a national park covering the northern gritstone moorlands (the Kinder and Bleaklow massifs and the moorlands east of the Derwent valley from Dunford Bridge to Ashopton) covering 205 square miles, together with Dovedale. The claims advanced in that proposal in favour of the Peak District were based on its ease of access to a large urban population, to its natural suitability to recreation, and to the fact that it was composed largely of uncultivated land. At that stage it was envisaged that the areas to be included in national parks would be 'nationalised' and in many quarters it was envisaged that instead of being the resort of intrepid trespassers and serious ramblers it would be over-run by parties from charabanc outings. Even Phil Barnes had his reservations about the high moorlands becoming a national park in these terms. He wrote to G.H.B. Ward in March 1930, having read the Manchester Ramblers' proposal for the Peak:

> *The great danger if the Peak becomes a N.P., to my mind, is the Snake Road running right through the centre of it, a road suitable for charabancs and with all those glorious cloughs, Fairbrook, Blackdean, the Alport etc. at the mercy of everybody who has a car and can walk a hundred yards. I am afraid I care for Kinder so much that I am perhaps taking a rather selfish view but, frankly, I would rather stay away from the hills myself and leave them to the tender mercies of the shooter and keeper, than see the delicate beauty of these cloughs vulgarised by picnic parties, as for instance the Conksbury Bridge end of the Lathkill, or the Thorpe end of the Dove, are today.*

In the event, the Addison Report of 1931 (Cmd. 3851) brought no tangible results other than to provide a platform for a lobby to pressurise the government.

In 1938 CPRE Headquarters reinforced Professor Abercrombie's advice and suggested that the time was ripe to revive the subject of a national park in the Peak District. The London Office also advised that membership of a committee considering a national park in the Peak District ought to go beyond the Sheffield and Peak District Branch and include representatives from other organisations such as the CPRE Derbyshire County and Buxton committees, the East Cheshire CPRE, the Staffordshire CPRE, the Ramblers' Federation, the Peak District Footpaths Society, suitable landowners and possibly planning officers.

It is interesting to note that Ethel wrote to H.G. Griffin, Joint Secretary of the CPRE Standing Committee on National Parks, in February 1938 to ask his opinion about the intention of the Government, in view of the heavy burden of administration and surveying that would have to done in order to assemble a sound case:

> *Before reviving this subject, and invoking the aid of the Manchester people, will you please advise me whether there is a reasonable chance of anything definite being done in the way of National Parks? I am ready to undertake a lot of work if this will be of real use, but naturally would avoid it otherwise. Are there grounds for thinking that a National Park in the Peak is a possibility in the next ten years?*

Griffin was absent from work having collapsed from overwork and although Ethel wrote again in March not knowing he was ill, the surviving correspondence contains no reply on the subject. Ethel pressed ahead and in September sent out invitations to about a dozen organisations to a meeting about the possibility of setting up a joint committee.

Griffin wrote to Ethel on 21 September 1938, saying that in the present state of national emergency it was extremely unlikely that the Government would take any action on national parks, and all they could do was to 'keep the subject warm and press it at every opportunity.' By 27 September he was being even more pessimistic:

> *Since I last wrote to you about this* [national parks], *the international situation has not improved and so far as Headquarters of the C.P.R.E. are concerned we have decided not to enter into any further commitments but to try to get our house in order, so as to be prepared for any emergency. In the circumstances, I think you would be well advised until we know exactly what is going to happen, to postpone the convening of a Conference about National Parks in the Peak.*

The CPRE might be considering shutting up shop, but Ethel pressed on. She convened a meeting at the Church Hotel, Edale on 19 November 1938, to which she invited Griffin, and John Dower, Drafting Secretary of the Standing Committee on National Parks. Griffin came on the clear understanding that he could not take sides (i.e. supporting one claim over another) and would only advise on matters of principle. The meeting was to be a private one and members of the press were to be excluded, a nominated delegate from the Manchester Ramblers' Federation, who was also a freelance reporter, having been thought to have leaked details (he denied it) to the *News Chronicle* (Manchester edition), much to the annoyance of Ethel, as it had upset various other parties involved in pushing the case for Dovedale as a national park. Ethel had made it known in her correspondence that she supported a scheme that would include Beeley and Abney Moors in the east and the limestone plateaus and dales to the west and linking them to the gritstone massifs to the north and ideally to Dovedale in the south to make a national park covering the whole of the Peak District. An indication of the feeling engendered when news of the proposed meeting was leaked came in a letter from Sir Robert McDougall, closely associated with a bid to make Dovedale a national park : 'Good wishes to the Peak–S. Yorkshire National Park but hands off the Dovedale National Park Scheme.' In a letter dated 25 October to D.M. Matheson, Secretary of the National Trust, Ethel made it clear that there was no question of interfering with the Dovedale scheme and competing for funds, concluding, in exasperation, 'I'm almost in the mood to scream at the word Dovedale!' She knew from Griffin's attitude that F.A. Holmes, of the Buxton Committee of the CPRE, and chief promoter of the Dovedale scheme, had been in touch with CPRE headquarters and in a letter dated 31 October she let Griffin know that she knew: 'I think I can see what has happened. Mr Holmes of Buxton has been active!' She also queried a statement made by Griffin in his letter to her of 29 October. In that letter he had said that if Ethel persisted in promoting a large national park in the Peak District which trespassed on the Dovedale scheme, the Dovedale promoters might 'invoke the Government report, and maintain that it referred to Dovedale as a possible National Park, but not to the Peak District...' Ethel's reply to this was very measured in view of the exasperation she must have felt:

> *I should greatly value more information on this matter. I have the report before me (April 1931) where on page 105 both the Peak District and Dovedale are listed as areas suggested as suitable for National Parks. Whereas two pages (72 & 73) are devoted to the Peak District case, only half a page (79)*

> *is devoted to Dovedale. Nowhere can I see any preference expressed for one or the other, but I may be mistaken. I have heard it said that the Peak District, including Dovedale, was among the first six areas considered suitable as National Parks. Is this true?*

Griffin subsequently blamed the speed with which he had dictated his letter for the false impression he had given.

The Edale meeting was attended by 42 people. In addition to the platform party (Ethel, Professor Forster, H.G. Griffin and John Dower) there were delegates representing CPRE branches from Sheffield and the Peak District, Derbyshire, East Cheshire and Staffordshire; Sheffield and Manchester Ramblers' Federations; the Peak District and Northern Counties Footpath Preservation Society; the Manchester & District Regional YHA Group; Sheffield Sub-Regional YHA Group; Derbyshire Rural Community Council; and Hallamshire Footpaths Society. Professor H.J. Fleure of Manchester University, Fred Marshall, MP and Captain H. Douglas, JP. were also there. The Buxton Area Committee of the CPRE did not send representatives, considering that their immediate effort should be devoted to the Dovedale scheme.

The chair was taken by Professor Forster and in his opening remarks (written by Ethel and vetted by H.G. Griffin and John Dower) he clearly laid down some guiding principles. The first was that by national park was not meant merely a national playground for townspeople. The question of greater access was very important, but 'the preservation of the Peak as an area of scenic value, whose rural nature should be permanently safeguarded and its farming encouraged, was of equal importance'. This statement was meant at one and the same time to encourage the rambling fraternity and to signal clearly the landscape preservation principle. He went on to emphasise that the organisers were well aware of the excellent proposals put forward in 1930. He also made it clear that there was no intention of interfering with the Dovedale scheme.

The opening remarks were then followed by a statement from John Dower. He pointed out that the CPRE could not champion any one proposal above any other: deciding about park designations was the role of a national park authority whose establishment was a priority. But he went on to say that those areas with worked-out schemes and organised local enthusiasm would stand the best chance. He then emphasised that the national parks campaign was a combination of three main streams of effort: landscape preservation, access and open-air recreation and protection of wildlife and that they were in equal association—there was no question of priority for one aspect over another. He then went on to make a number of personal statements. He said he put the Peak District and Dovedale (which he regarded as a single unit for national park purposes) high on the list for national park status because of their intrinsic merit and because of the large surrounding urban populations. He trusted they would go right ahead and form a joint committee. He trusted they would continue their efforts with unabated vigour but in combination and with thorough co-ordination and produce a thoroughly worked out, agreed scheme discussed with the planning authorities. Only then should it be made public: 'when you have a full and consistent story to tell, tell it with all your might.'

Three resolutions were passed unanimously at the meeting:

> *That the meeting considered it desirable that the Peak District, north and east of the Dovedale area should become a National Park, on the understanding that this project is undertaken in complete sympathy with the Dovedale National Park scheme, but separate from it.*
>
> *That the area to be included in the proposed National Park for the Peak District shall be, roughly speaking, that shown by the dotted black line on the Map, on view at this Meeting, and that details of this area shall be worked out later.*
>
> *That an ad hoc Joint Committee to further the object of a National Park for the Peak District be formed under the auspices of the Sheffield & Peak District Branch of the C.P.R.E....*

Ethel was appointed Honorary Secretary.

The first meeting of the Committee took place on 28 January 1939, again at the Church Hotel at Edale. Ethel had suggested to Griffin and Dower that they should become members of the Joint Committee. Griffin declined because he thought he ought to be neutral; John Dower agreed to be the honorary technical consultant to the Committee. The main business of the meeting was the setting up of sub-committees of local experts to examine in more detail the boundaries of the proposed national park and to suggest amendments to those shown on the provisional map presented at the meeting in the previous November. Mr A.J. Radcliff of Ughill Hall, Bradfield, agreed to look in detail at the section from Bradfield to Holmfirth; Mr T. Boulger of the Peak District Footpaths Preservation Society, W.P. Hunt of the Sheffield & Peak District Branch of the CPRE, and A.W. Hewitt of the Manchester & District Ramblers' Federation were asked to examine the boundary from Holmfirth to Whaley

Bridge; Miss D.M. Pilkington of the East Cheshire Branch of the CPRE was asked to comment on the boundary in the west from Whaley Bridge to Dawe Bridge (where the Dovedale scheme began); Mr V.H. Jowitt, Stanley Meyrick and Mr H. Mutton were asked to examine the southern and south-eastern and boundaries; and Ethel and Gerald looked in detail at the boundary from Tansley to Bradfield, with comments from Mr. S. Morton, of the Sheffield & District Ramblers' Federation, Mr A.C. Panter of the Hallamshire Footpaths Society and Mr F. Turton of the YHA Sheffield Sub-Regional Council. The amended map was discussed at the second meeting of the Joint Committee at the Nag's Head, Edale on 17 June 1939. The problematic areas were in the south-east where there was debate about whether to include areas of 'Midlands' rather than 'Pennine' character, in the east where the East Cheshire Branch decided to remove the Cheshire section west of the Goyt valley because it was unhappy about how a future national park would be managed, but were subsequently placated by John Dower; and the spoiled areas around Whaley Bridge, Buxton, Wirksworth and the Matlocks.

After the June meeting, when time permitted over the summer and autumn, in spite of the declaration of war, Ethel showed the map to various planning officials and members of local authorities known to be sympathetic, to get their reaction and advice. All this took place outside the public gaze and without the knowledge of the press. The annual reports of the Branch for 1939 and 1940 simply indicate that work was in progress.

V

In spite of the over-riding importance of the Sheffield Green Belt campaign, the 'Save the Countryside' Exhibition and the work of the Joint Committee for the Peak District National Park, the period 1936–39 saw the Branch continuing to assume the mantle of watchdog over the same wide range of affairs as it had done over the previous twelve years.

Road improvements and their possible effects on old bridges continued to occupy much time. In September 1936 it was reported that the proposed Bakewell by-pass would involve the creation of a 160 feet-wide road through the river pastures, the canalising of the River Wye in places, and almost cutting into the old packhorse bridge and the town bridge. It was being opposed by Bakewell Urban District Council who had requested the support of the Branch at a public inquiry. Gerald wrote an article with a map in *Derbyshire Countryside* and 500 copies of the article were printed and distributed. The problem then disappeared for the time being.

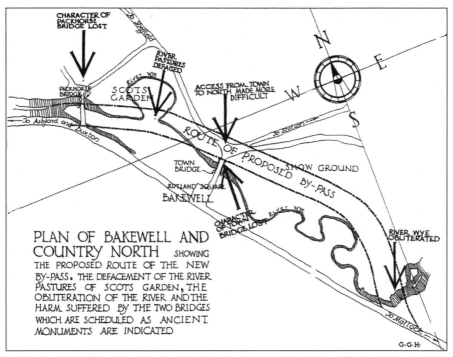

Map by Gerald Haythornthwaite showing the impact of the proposed Bakewell by- pass.

But a worse possible catastrophe was revealed in January 1938 in the form of another proposal to make a motor road through the Winnats. At the March 1938 Executive Committee meeting a long discussion took place about how to counter this threat. Representatives from the Peak District and Northern Counties Footpaths Preservation Society and the Manchester Ramblers' Federation took part in the discussion. It was finally decided to ask for a Ministry of Transport representative to accompany a deputation from the Branch on an inspection of the site. On 6 July 1938 an inquiry took place at which in support of the opposition to the proposal, Professor Husband suggested that instead of up-grading the Winnats Pass route, the existing Mam Tor road could be rendered secure by re-building it on concrete piers. The proposal was dismissed. Subsequently, Ethel approached the owner of the Winnats with a view to its being acquired for the National Trust, but she was told it was not for sale.

The subject of disfiguring advertisements and garish petrol stations also continued to receive attention. Petrol station bye-laws for the West Riding were sent for approval to the Home Office by the West Riding County Council in the autumn of 1936, but there was unease at the Branch

The Winnats.

because the bye-laws did not cover existing stations. Additionally, although stations were prohibited in a large portion of the Moscar, Strines and Langsett areas, there was no such provision for Ecclesfield and Tankersley parishes.

There was also continued concern at the laxity of Derbyshire County Council over the application of its advertisement bye-laws, and the growing number of large posters that were still appearing all over the Peak District. At the Executive Meeting held in December 1936, it was reported that 80 bad examples had been reported to the Peak Planning Committee who had in turn reported them to the County Council but no action had yet been forthcoming. Among the 80 examples cited was an advertisement for Treak Cliff Cavern, cut in huge letters on the slopes of Mam Tor. Later that year a resolution was sent to the County Council together with the Annual Report which contained photographs of blatant examples of inappropriately placed advertisements. The Clerk of the Council had written to say that certain advertisements were being inspected and that the matter would receive early attention. By December ten particularly bad cases of disfiguring advertising had been removed.

On the industrial front, the main focus was on Edale. At the March 1937 Executive Committee meeting it was reported that under the powers of the Petroleum Production Act of 1934, Steel Brothers of London had been given a licence to search for oil in North-west Derbyshire including Edale and the Snake valley, Longshaw, Burbage and Ringinglow. Ethel had been informed that a preliminary boring was to take place near Barber Booth in Edale. In May a meeting was held at Endcliffe Vale House with officials of the Peak Joint Planning Committee and a representative from Messrs Steel Brothers. By March 1938 it was clear that oil would not be found in commercial quantities and the problem went away.

But it was almost immediately replaced by another major scare in the same area. In April 1939 the Executive Committee received confirmation of a rumour that Brown Bayley's of Sheffield proposed to erect a steelworks on land adjoining the disused mill in Edale. In the words of the Annual Report for 1940 this would mean ' the ruin of the heart of the Peak, and thereby the Peak itself. It would shatter all hope of a National Park, and virtually undo the fourteen years' efforts of the Branch.'

Despite the fact that 172 letters of protest and nine telegrams were sent to the local authority concerned—Chapel-en-le Frith—and that the Sheffield and Manchester press were deluged with correspondence, the local authority on 1 May sanctioned the proposal under the mistaken impression that the Government was particularly anxious that a steelworks should be set up on the Edale site.

Influential allies in Parliament were mobilised and 200 MPs of all parties signed a petition against the proposal and letters were published in *The Times*. Sheffield City Council passed a unanimous resolution against the proposal. On 10 May the Branch arranged a deputation to speak to the directors of Brown Bayley's. Subsequently the Minister of Health and the Air Minister met the Brown Bayley directors to discuss alternative sites. By the end of the month the threat had evaporated.

It was noted at the July 1939 Executive Meeting that the expansion of the lime industry was probably the most serious problem confronting the effort to safeguard Peak scenery—a very prescient remark in view of what was to happen in the post-war years.

Two issues that assumed prominence in the 1936–39 period, having only appeared very briefly in Executive Meeting minutes in the previous twelve years, were tree management and tree planting. In January 1936 the Branch was asked to prepare a map for the Forestry Commission indicating the areas in the Peak District where it was thought any planting of conifers was undesirable. The Branch also urged the Derwent Valley Water Board, that if new planting was necessary, to plant native hardwoods instead of conifers. There was also concern over the treatment of trees in Sheffield in 1938 and 1939, when trees had been unnecessarily felled in Stumperlowe Road, and others drastically lopped in Fulwood Road and elsewhere. Concern was also expressed in 1939 over the planting of exotics instead of native shrubs on the central reservation of the Taddington by-pass, out of keeping with the limestone scenery. The planting turned out to have been directed by the Roads Beautifying Association which was asked to consult with the Branch in future when roadside tree planting in the Peak District was being considered.

The work of the Advisory Panel of Architects went on unabated. In 1936 the booklet *Small Houses and Bungalows Suitable for the Peak District* was published and widely distributed. The Panel continued to be heavily used by several local authorities including Penistone and Wortley Rural District Councils. The panel also assisted in 1937 and 1938 in the RIBA survey of small farms and cottages, with a view to scheduling those of architectural, historical or aesthetic merit against indiscriminate demolition orders. The Panel began with those in the Porter Valley recently condemned by the Sheffield Medical Officer of Health.

Finally, the 1936–39 period was one in which a number of important purchases of land were made, either because of their beauty or because they were threatened with development. Ethel and the rest of the Ward family were heavily involved in all but one of these purchases. In September 1936, 250 acres of land below the Surprise View was handed over to the National Trust. This extension to the Longshaw estate had been purchased by the Longshaw Committee following an appeal for £7,000 which had resulted in 800 people subscribing, with amounts ranging from sixpence to £1,000. Shortly afterwards an anonymous friend of the Branch and Longshaw purchased Whim Plantation and Harpur Lees Farm in order to preserve permanently in its rural state land adjoining the Longshaw estate on the north and west. In 1938, £3,000 was raised by Ethel in a few days to purchase 76 acres below Froggatt Edge, including Froggatt Wood, the property again being presented to the National Trust. In 1939, with the generous help of her brother, Alan, Ethel purchased 75 acres of farmland at Shatton where building was threatened.

VI

The four years from 1936 to 1939 were momentous years for the Branch, but at the very point when the momentum was with them, there was a danger that everything would have to stop. But Ethel refused to succumb to the general feeling of despondency. She was on her own again from September 1939 when Gerald was called up with his Territorial unit but she realised that the price of the preservation of rural scenery of England in general and the Peak District in particular was eternal vigilance. She wrote about this very openly to her friend Joan Batten at the end of November:

> *When war was impending the general feeling was, I think, that we should all be in chaos by reason of air raids during the first few weeks. This may well happen yet, of course, but as civilian life is still fairly normal, I think unquestionably the C.P.R.E. and all its Branches should strive their best to hold on. If not, much more of England's beauty will be lost for those who return after the war, or for those who must carry on the country even over all our dead bodies. I never thought myself of letting go till we really <u>must</u>. I believe our aims are too profoundly important for that. And while most healthy women can do some kind of emergency work, there are only such a limited number who see what rural England means to the English, and therefore would work to save it.*

Major Gerald Haythornthwaite on active service.

4

The war years

1940–1944

I

AS THE STORM CLOUDS darkened in the autumn of 1939, it was not clear what work the Branch should or would be able to undertake in wartime. If there were an invasion, then concerns and efforts would be elsewhere and work would have to be suspended, but if the war were fought largely or wholly outside Britain, it was Ethel's view that the campaign to protect the Peak District scenery should and would go on as before in some modified form—what was called in the 1941 Annual Report 'daily diligence and constant vigilance'. It was realised that private and local authority housing developments would virtually come to a standstill, and that there would be rationing. The first would ease the burden of monitoring and advising on building styles and use of materials, and the second would provide a golden opportunity to get rid of intrusive and disfiguring advertisements by commercial firms along country roads and at petrol stations. On the other hand, industrial developments and government building in connection with the war effort were more than likely, and the national interest would almost certainly over-ride local and regional objections on conservation grounds.

In the event, the Branch remained very busy and in the Annual Report for 1944, Ethel was able to report that the Branch had rarely been more active. About 200 new members joined during the war years and by mid-1944 membership was approaching 1000. Ethel's reputation was such that in 1942 she was co-opted to the CPRE-administered Standing Committee on National Parks. On top of her local work, Ethel also agreed in the spring of 1942 to spend three days each week at the London office of the CPRE deputising for H.G. Griffin, who was absent on military duties. She did this for seven months. This must have put her under much strain, but it also enabled her to secure national prominence.

Ethel riding her horse Bracken in her beloved 'stone country'.

II

Throughout the war years the issue of the Sheffield Green Belt and town and country planning within Sheffield City Council's boundaries in general were constant topics of concerned discussion at Executive Committee meetings, and matters on which it was considered necessary to make periodic representations. The general perception of the public, in the view of Ethel and the members of the Executive Committee, was that the Green Belt was an established fact. But the Executive knew this was not the case. The City Council needed to be reminded about being vigilant and about honouring its commitments. On the one hand it was thought that attention would be diverted to other issues and that the Green Belt might be gradually eaten into in the west and south and possibly destroyed altogether in the east where it was already discontinuous; on the other hand, because the Green Belt was provisional and had no legal protection, there were fears that the City Council itself might acquire land and later develop it.

At the March 1940 Executive Meeting it was reported that the Town Clerk had stated that there was no intention of jeopardising the Green Belt scheme, though it was known that two planning officers who had previously been involved full time on the scheme were now employed for some of their time on other planning issues. In September it was reported that the City Council had recently acquired 29 acres in the Gleadless area, the 117-acre Abbeydale Golf Course and land at Whirlow Grange for the construction of a new road. It was minuted that this was probably due to 'a desire to consolidate the scheme, but there was always the danger that some of the land purchased might be later used for development'. Further alarm bells rang in March 1941 when it was reported to the Executive Committee that the 53-acre Totley Hall Farm, within the Green Belt, had been advertised for sale. The Branch encouraged the Council to purchase it, but the response was that money was hard to obtain and anyway there was little danger of development because there were no utilities on the site. At the same meeting the possibilities of a 'reconstructed Sheffield on sound lines after the war' was also discussed, but it was concluded that the outlook was 'not at all hopeful', especially as Alderman Marshall had decided not to put up for the Council again.

Concern that incursions into the Green Belt would occur, and that insufficient time would be available to marshal concerted action was borne out by the decision to site a war factory north of the Don near Middlewood Road in the north-western part of the proposed Green Belt, 'that long-suffering region' as Ethel called it. The factory was authorised by the Government, and although the Corporation protested, City Council officials failed to inform local MPs, or the CPRE. The Executive Committee believed, in view of its previous successes, that it could have successfully urged an alternative site. This *fait accompli* prompted the Branch to send a letter to the Town Clerk at the end of June 1941, signed by Professor Forster, Dr Bramley, Sir Samuel Osborn, Lord Riverdale and G.H.B. Ward, asking that in future the Branch might be informed immediately of any threat to the Green Belt, and asking that the letter be brought to the attention of the next meeting of the Special Town Planning Committee. The reply from the Town Clerk that 'he felt sure his Committee would do their best to keep the Branch fully informed of developments of a permanent character' within the Green Belt, was felt to be unsatisfactory and it was decided that a further letter should be sent. At the meeting of the Executive Committee in October 1941, it was reported that it had been learnt that the first letter sent in June had never been brought before the Special Town Planning

Committee as requested and that there had been no response to a second request sent in August. Dr Bramley had been informed confidentially that 'the official view was not unfavourable to the CPRE', but that the difficulty lay with certain members of the Planning Committee. It was decided to approach individual members of the Committee and ask them 'point blank' for their opinion on the matter. Meanwhile, the Council continued to purchase land in the Green Belt. By April 1942, the 75-acre Barber Fields Farm on Long Line, Yarncliff Farm in the upper Porter Valley and Ryecroft Farm at Dore had been acquired, but, while applauding these acquisitions in public, privately the Executive Committee counselled 'watchfulness lest any of these acquisitions be used for housing development'.

The relationship of Sheffield to the wider region, especially in relation to its green belt policy, was a focus for debate at Executive Committee meetings on various occasions between 1940 and 1943 under the headings of local, regional and national planning. The tone of the minutes was gloomy and pessimistic. In the view of the Executive Committee, there was a lack of vision, clarity and leadership in the City Council. While supporting the principle of a green belt, it was understood that there was a proposal to build 10,000 more houses in the Norton, Greenhill and Bradway districts, and 20,000 in the neighbourhood of Handsworth and Woodhouse; after that building might be extended over the city boundary on the south-east in the Frecheville and Hackenthorpe direction. There were also fears from Chesterfield Rural District Council that Sheffield would over-run its green belt in the south and lose the confidence of the Dronfield and Chesterfield authorities, who sympathised with the Sheffield Green Belt scheme. There was a 'persistent fear' that the 250-acre Hazlebarrow Farm would be sacrificed to 'ill-advised suburban extension'.

It was decided to try to arrange a regional planning conference in Sheffield during 1943. This took place on 6 March. The speakers in the 'Town' session were Dr Dudley Stamp, Director of the Land Utilisation Survey, on 'Agriculture and Green Belts', and John Dower on 'Recreation and the Countryside'; the 'Country' session featured F.J. Osborn of the Town and Country Planning Association, speaking on 'The Future of Industrial Towns' and G.A. Jellicoe on 'Rebuilding Cities and Civic Design'. More than twenty local authorities sent representatives. In opening the 'Town' session, the Lord Mayor of Sheffield, Councillor Bridgwater, emphasised that there should be no encroachment on the Green Belt. Despite the qualified success of the conference, it was felt that local authorities, however sympathetic to the general principles of local and regional planning, were hampered by a lack of a national planning framework. In September 1943 it was agreed to write to CPRE headquarters to express concern, and to support any measures to induce government action on the basis of the Barlow (1940), Scott (1942) and Uthwatt (1942) reports. The Scott Committee advocated the creation of a central planning body, the maintenance of prosperous farming, the preservation of rural amenities, and the resuscitation of village and country life. In the Annual Report for 1943, Ethel wrote that it was 'almost a charter for the CPRE'. The Uthwatt Committee had gone even further, arguing for the establishment of mechanisms to implement land-use planning.

In March 1944 another letter was sent to the Town Clerk asking for an assurance that the 1938 Green Belt scheme would be adhered to. Again the response was equivocal: 'subject to their due discharge of their obligations in other respects and to over-riding considerations which may from time to time prevail, the Town Planning Committee will do their best to secure the Green Belt plan which has been provisionally approved by the City Council.' It was decided to send a letter to the press and to endeavour to produce a pamphlet to influence and inform public opinion on the subject. Wallace Hunt, ARIBA, AMTPI, agreed to write the pamphlet and take a number of new photographs to illustrate the text.

The year 1944 ended with two successful campaigns. In the summer of 1944 the owner of Fulwood Hall in the upper Porter Valley proposed to develop Green Belt land surrounding the Hall which was greeted by the public, according to the Annual Report for 1945 'with surprise and the warmest indignation'. Despite protests from the Executive Committee, the Town Planning Committee, although refusing permission to build on the hillcrest behind the Hall, did not refuse permission to build on fifteen acres to the north of the Hall. The would-be developer rejected the offered partial permission from the City Council and appealed to the Ministry of Town and Country Planning for permission to build on the whole site. This led to a public inquiry in November 1944 at which a petition with over 3,000 signatures was handed to the inspector. The case for the CPRE was put by Mr P.M. Oliver. The would-be developer's proposal was duly dismissed by the Ministry of Town and Country Planning. At the same time that the upper Porter Valley was being threatened by incompatible residential development, Bowden Housteads Wood, a valued open space in the east of the City of Sheffield, was threatened with destruction through open-cast mining for coal. The Branch, together with the City Council and local MPs, objected in the strongest terms to the Ministries of Fuel & Power, and Town and Country Planning, and a decision was deferred.

Higger Tor.

III

Having outlined the boundaries of a national park for the Peak District in the months immediately preceding the outbreak of war, including bearing in mind the sensitivities of those promoting a separate scheme for Dovedale, it was to be expected that in the first part of the war no further progress towards national park designation would be made and matters would become dormant. But not quite. Ethel not only continued to talk through the boundary proposals with selected 'sympathetic' planning officers and local councillors, but—and this seems quite extraordinary in hindsight—as early as April 1940 she had drawn up a proposal for the form and content of a leaflet about a Peak District National Park and circulated it for comment. In her letter she said

> *Although no steps are likely to be taken by the government to further National Parks during wartime, it has seemed best nevertheless to prepare a draft of this leaflet now, so that when the appropriate time comes, we may lose no ground, but be prepared to issue it at once.*

By July 1940, largely through the wise intervention of John Dower and a conciliatory meeting with Ethel in Manchester, the East Cheshire Branch of the CPRE had withdrawn its objections to the inclusion of the Pennine areas of their region within the proposed Peak District National Park boundary. It was worried that national park status would mean access for all and sundry on private land; it was persuaded that at this stage in the campaign it was more to do with preservation of scenery.

But on another front, reconciliation proved to be as difficult as ever. On 17 June 1942 Ethel wrote to F.A. Holmes, the chief promoter of national park status for Dovedale, and implacably opposed to combining the Dovedale claim with that of the rest of the Peak District. Ethel must have had grounds for assuming that the time was propitious to sound him out about combining the two proposals. She had become a member of the Standing Committee on National Parks, had begun working at the London headquarters of the CPRE, had enlarged her circle of contacts, and she had continued to be in contact with John Dower, now with the Ministry of Works and Planning and who was to become a close confidant of Lord Reith, the Minister of Town and Country Planning. In her letter to Holmes she said the time seemed to have come when it seemed not only highly desirable but also essential for both parties to help each other to go forward in a combined scheme. She went on:

*From information I have, I am encouraged to believe that
both our hopes are not unjustified. But I have been given to
understand that small areas alone are not what is required,
and therefore, for every reason, we do most earnestly hope
that we can co-operate with you in urging a scheme that will
embrace what we both desire.*

She concluded by saying that she hoped he would consider her proposal
favourably 'for it appears to me—though I write in deference to your longer
experience—that if we work apart, we may both damage or even ruin our
respective aspirations.'

Holmes wrote back to Ethel immediately and went straight into the case
for Dovedale without any of the normal courtesies. He reiterated that Dovedale
had been placed in 'the first category' by the National Parks Report (1931)
for 'specific, scientific, educational, and recreational reasons.' He went on
to emphasise the distinctiveness of Dovedale and said he had no hesitation
in his mind that the Standing Committee on National Parks would agree to
there being two national parks in Derbyshire. He went on to state that the
daily, evening, weekly and monthly press had come out unanimously in
their favour, and that there was large-scale support from the general public
including a preservation society in the United States with 60,000 members
supporting the claims of Dovedale. He said merging the Dovedale claim
with the rest of the Peak District would be ungenerous and callous to the
memory of Sir Robert McDougall who had given nearly £30,000 for the
purchase of land in Dovedale and had spent so many years of his life on its
behalf. He said he did not agree with Ethel that if they worked apart both
schemes would be damaged. He wished her good luck with her scheme ('it
will be quite safe in your hands') and ended by stating that 'We stand and
fall by the Dovedale scheme. THE NATION WILL SEE TO THAT.'

Ethel subsequently sent copies of both her letter and Holmes' reply to
John Dower and D.M. Matheson, Secretary of the National Trust.

In October 1942 the first meeting of the Voluntary Joint Committee for
the Peak National Park since 1939 took place at the St James' Club in
Sheffield. John Dower attended the meeting. The first part of the meeting
was concerned with bringing members up to date with issues such as
boundaries, interviews with 'friendly' planning officers (who had not
informed their councils about what was happening), and disfigurement by
the limestone quarrying industry. The second part, in which John Dower
played a significant role, was concerned with 'the present position'. He
stated that he had been instructed to inspect the first six areas proposed as
national parks by the Standing Committee on National Parks and to make

a report to his Ministry. He was beginning his inspection of the Peak District that weekend. Referring to the intransigence of F.A. Holmes over the Dovedale issue, Dower said that his instructions were to investigate the Peak with Dovedale, and that the latter would probably be considered too small on its own. He considered the Scott Report to be 'altogether on our side, particularly the Ramblers' side, and was our propaganda'. Under future action, it was decided that a small illustrated booklet propounding the need for a national park in the Peak District, should be prepared ready for publication when war conditions made this possible.

A further meeting was held in Manchester in October 1943. The main items on the agenda were, first, the revision of the boundaries to reduce the area of the proposed Peak District National Park from 700 to 600 square miles. This was on advice (presumably from Ethel via John Dower) that a smaller area would be more likely to succeed. Secondly, came the not unexpected announcement that the Dovedale campaigners had once more rejected overtures about co-operation. It was decided that every possible effort had been made on their side and that henceforth the Committee 'must proceed on its own lines as it deemed best.' Finally, it was reported that a revised draft booklet had been sent to Mr Symonds, Hon. Drafting Secretary to the Standing Committee on National Parks and his suggested amendments had been largely adopted. It was resolved to publish the booklet as soon as possible, at the expense of the Sheffield and Peak District Branch of the CPRE. A print run of 5,000 was agreed with a projected publication date in the spring or summer of 1944.

In the meantime the Dovedale question refused to go away and it was reported at the next Joint Committee meeting held in Manchester in February 1944 that the Dovedale Committee had upset the National Trust by suggesting in an article in the press that it was pursuing its campaign 'in harmony with the committee of the National Trust'. The National Trust sent a letter to the press, intimating that the Trust was in favour of Dovedale being included in a bigger national park scheme for the Peak District, but this was abbreviated so that the opposite meaning was implied. This resulted in the National Trust suggesting that the Joint Committee should write to the Trust asking for an explanation of its position, so that the Trust could reply in writing, it being understood that the letter could be published by the Joint Committee if necessary. The letter emphasised the National Trust's support for one national park in the Peak District, roughly coinciding with the Joint Committee's mapped area plus Dovedale and the Manifold Valley:

> *It is not the business of the National Trust to select what should*
> *be National Parks, but it seems to it that, if a National Park*
> *is set up in the Midlands, it would be much better to have one*

*National Park which would include not only the wild moorlands
between Sheffield, Huddersfield and Manchester, but also the
country in and around Dovedale, and the Manifold Valley,
and other parts of the beautiful country which lies roughly
within the area between Huddersfield, Sheffield, Derby,
Ashbourne and Manchester. We feel that it would be a great
pity and a mistaken policy if a number of National Parks were
set up in this one area, which is of such great social importance
to a very large industrial population.*

The booklet *The Peak District A National Park* was published at the end
of May 1944. In terms of content and timing it was a brilliant piece of advocacy
and propaganda. On turning over the front cover, which contained only the
title, the price and the phrase 'To all who love the Peak country' the reader
was confronted by not one *coup de théâtre*, but two. On the inside cover was
a Foreword by Lord Justice Scott, author of the hugely influential Scott Report
of 1942 which had given its wholehearted support to the policy of national
parks. The Foreword contained the phrase 'it [the Peak District] *must* be one
of the first National Parks to be created by Parliament'. On the opposite page
was a full-page map of the area of the Peak District National Park as
recommended by the Joint Committee, with the boundary, including Dovedale
and the Manifold Valley, outlined in red. The text was concerned with both
national parks in general and the Peak District in particular, and was both
informative and polemical. Four carefully chosen photographs, including one
of the Ilam Rock in Dovedale, decorated the text. A particularly crucial
passage, in the section concerned with the case for a national park in the Peak
District, dealt with the issue of the geographical position of the Peak District
in relation to surrounding towns and cities, compared to those areas which
were remote and not in danger of destruction. The passage appears to be
throwing down the gauntlet to central government. The passage runs:

*...the choice or rejection of the Peak District as a National
Park will indicate what, in the mind of the Government, is to
be the fundamental principle of post-war planning. Will the
choice fall on regions by nature unproductive, by situation
remote from industry, regions indeed in comparatively slight
danger of spoliation, or on those reservoirs of spiritual and
physical health which still exist on the borders of densely
populated areas and which are in imminent danger through
harmful development? Naturally, the preservation of both
types is of vital importance, but it is in the choice or rejection
of the latter that the public will be made aware whether or*

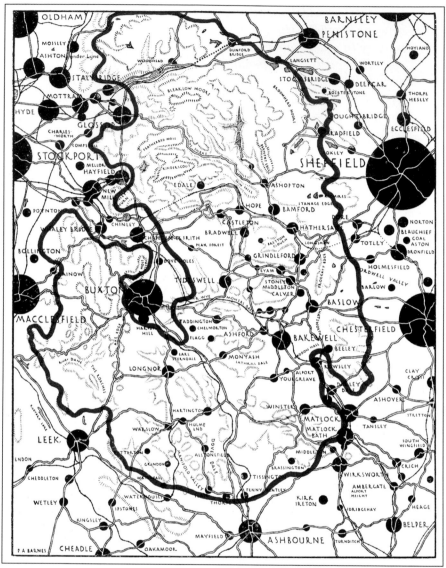

Area of the proposed Peak District National Park as recommended by the Voluntary Joint Committee and published in The Peak District A National Park *in 1944.*

*no its true welfare will take precedence of material convenience
and private gain.*

The booklet was distributed widely, received a good press especially in
the *Sheffield Telegraph*, *Manchester Guardian* and *Observer*, and aroused
considerable interest among MPs. The first printing of 5,000 copies was
disposed of in a few weeks and a second impression of a further 5,700
copies was issued in July. Its publication preceded by less than a year the
publication of John Dower's report on *National Parks in England and
Wales* (April 1945), followed closely by the appointment of Sir Arthur
Hobhouse by the new Labour government as chairman of a Committee on
National Parks in England and Wales, charged with making specific
recommendations arising out of the Dower Report. Ethel was appointed a
member of the Hobhouse Committee. She was in the box seat and the Peak
District looked likely to be in the vanguard of national park designations.

Ancient field boundaries in the White Peak.

Eldon Hill Quarry.

IV

While campaigning for a national park in the Peak District went on and boundary disputes continued, attention was kept on what was seen to be the greatest threat to the landscape in the White Peak, especially in the Hope Valley and at Eldon Hill—quarrying for limestone and the associated cement works. In early 1940 Ethel visited the various sites in the company of H.G. Griffin, and they called on A.L. Oldacre, the planning officer of the Peak Joint Planning Committee. Although sharing their concern, Oldacre was of the opinion that the only way to stop further encroachments was by compensation from the National Exchequer, which was unlikely as the works were working at full capacity for the war effort. In May 1940 Ethel, again in the company of Griffin and Oldacre, had a meeting with senior personnel of ICI but few concessions were made. They stated that there was no hope of the Hindlow works being curtailed, the demand for the war effort being enormous; nor could they change their tipping methods (which were spoiling skylines) which were based on the best way of working their quarries from one end to another. On the positive side they did intimate that they had no intention of extending their workings around Buxton or of re-opening their property above Miller's Dale. In October 1941 Ethel went with Fred Marshall and F.W. Scorah to see representatives of the Derbyshire Stone Company. The firm had begun working the hillside west of Earle's Works and were starting to quarry in Pindale. They were asked if they would abandon the Pindale quarry after the war but they refused. The situation there was subsequently described as 'hopeless'.

At the end of 1941 a meeting was held at CPRE headquarters in London between George Earle and a deputation from the Branch consisting of Ethel and Fred Marshall, and from the CPRE National Executive in the persons of H.G. Griffin and Professor Patrick Abercrombie. Its object was to seek re-assurances against unrestricted encroachment of limestone quarrying in the proposed Peak District National Park area. Subsequently a larger deputation went to the works at Hope to discuss returfing, planting and general amelioration of defacement with the works manager. The notes made by Ethel on the meeting were not accepted by the manager. After the meeting Fred Marshall had led a deputation to George Hicks, Parliamentary Secretary to Lord Reith, at which facts about the detrimental impact of the Hope Valley Cement Works on the proposed National Park area were presented. Ethel also sent a memorandum to the Scott Committee.

G.A. Jellicoe, President of the Institute of Landscape Architects, had promised, if invited by Earle's, to visit the Hope Valley Cement Works in the autumn of 1942. The visit took place in October. Also present were George Earle, H.G. Griffin, a Mr Dodds representing the Ministry of Works and Planning, and Professor F.C. Lea, representing the Branch. Jellicoe produced a report, which constituted a set of long-term recommendations for counteracting the worst features of intrusion and disfigurement. The main recommendations were that the entrance to the quarry should be kept narrow, with the quarry worked fanwise from it and the summit kept below the skyline. With regard to waste, the horizontal lines should be adjusted to adjoining slopes, new waste should fill the adjoining quarry and recreate the original hillside, top soil to be provided and the whole grassed over to match the existing hill. The clay excavations should be treated as lakes or planted with hardwoods and there should be research into the final elimination of white steam. A letter was sent to the Branch by George Earle stating that the firm intended to go forward on the lines of the report with two exceptions: the treatment to the entrance of their quarry and further elimination of steam.

In the winter of 1943 Earle's proposed to establish a large cement works at Caldon Low, Waterhouses, near the southern entrance to the Manifold Valley, on the borders of the proposed Peak District National Park. The Branch decided to employ Mr P.M. Oliver to oppose the proposals at the public inquiry held at Cheadle in November 1944. Although opposed by the CPRE, the Standing Committee on National Parks, the National Trust, Staffordshire County Council, Stoke Corporation and all local amenity societies, the local community was strongly in favour of the proposal because of local unemployment. In March 1945 the Minister of Planning announced that he had granted permission for the new works, subject to certain conditions to safeguard local amenities.

V

The other major threat to the Peak scenery was the creation of reservoirs and associated waterworks. In late 1940 and in early 1941 the Derwent Valley Water Board Bill, which proposed far-reaching control over the Edale Valley, occupied a great deal of Branch time. The main features of the bill were the proposed construction of a collecting pool formed by a dam across the River Noe below Nether Booth, an open aqueduct between this pool and Jagger's Clough, an aqueduct tunnelled under Win Hill, and pipelines alongside the River Ashop to Ladybower Reservoir. The Branch supported the proposal provided there were certain safeguards, i.e. that the farming character of the Dale was safeguarded, the aqueducts were taken underground, that footpaths should be maintained in their present unfenced condition, and that any necessary buildings were in the local stone and traditional style. The National Trust also petitioned on similar grounds, and was successful in getting the Board to agree to put the aqueduct from the collecting pool to Jagger's Clough underground. The other conditions put forward by the Branch were supported by Chapel Rural District Council and the County Council. In the event the Bill was withdrawn, but was revived in 1943–44 when the earlier concessions were again granted and the character of the valley safeguarded.

As the Ladybower Reservoir scheme neared completion in late 1942, the Branch made recommendations about the appearance of the parapet walls, about the possibility of substituting concrete posts and wire fencing with local stone, about road surfaces, and about tree planting. At first the Derwent Valley Water Board did not act. This was doubly disappointing because in the case of earlier schemes the Board had consulted the Branch about materials in order to ensure that the finished undertaking would be in harmony with and not alien to its scenic setting. It was decided to approach the Ministry of Planning and to write letters to the press. A letter signed by the Branch President, Chairman, Fred Marshall, Ethel and Major Douglas of the Peak Planning Committee was published in *The Times* and nine other newspapers in April 1942. The Duke of Devonshire, who was Lord Lieutenant of the County, thought he might be able to influence the Water Board and he arranged to accompany another deputation from the Branch in May 1942. By 1944 it was reported in the Annual Report that the Parliamentary Secretary to the Ministry of Transport had given instructions for thorn hedges to be planted at the end of the war to screen the ten miles of concrete and wire fences.

In 1944 it was proposed by Leicester Corporation to construct a large reservoir, two and a half miles in length and breadth, between Longnor and Brund Mill in the Upper Manifold Valley, involving the submerging of 24 farmsteads and the flooding of 950 acres of excellent farmland. Professor Joseph Husband was retained by the Voluntary Joint Committee for the Peak National Park as consultant and he suggested that the extraction of water from the River Trent should be considered as an alternative to the expensive construction of a large reservoir and a pipeline more than 50 miles long. The matter was not resolved until 1946.

Marsh House in the Manifold Valley, a farm producing milk for Stilton cheese, threatened by submergence by the proposed construction of a reservoir by Leicester Corporation.

VI

The Branch was active during the war years whenever opportunities arose in acquiring key landmarks and sites under threat in the Peak District. In December 1940, through the generosity of Ethel's brother, Alan Ward, it had been possible to provide a loan to the National Trust so that two farms, both in Edale, comprising 300 acres in all, could be purchased. With the help of a legacy, the Trust had been able to pay off the loan. The farms in question were Lees Farm and adjoining cottage under the eastern bluffs of Kinder Scout, and Orchard Farm under Horsehill Tor. In early 1942 another Edale farm, Edale End Farm, a 91-acre hill farm with coppice wood at the foot of Jaggers Clough on the eastern slopes of Kinder Scout, came onto the market and, believing it could be affected detrimentally by the Derwent Valley Water Board and knowing the National Trust was keen to acquire it but did not have the means to do so, Ethel used a sum of money given to her by her brother Alan for CPRE purposes, to buy the farm and present it to the National Trust. This was done on the understanding that the Trust would use all the means in its power to secure the preservation of all the farms at the lower end of Edale, which was the part of the valley most vulnerable to development.

What remained of Alan Ward's generous gift of money to be used for CPRE purposes was spent in 1942 on the purchase of half a mile of road frontage (28 acres) in Upper Middleton Dale near Eyam to prevent further quarrying in that direction. The owner of the opposite frontage, Lord Denman, though not willing to make a binding agreement, had let it be known that his property would not be allowed to be exploited for quarrying.

The greatest acquisition during the war years for the National Trust was undoubtedly that of Mam Tor and the neighbouring Winnats, 473 acres in all, in late 1943. The purchase was made possible by a legacy left by Miss Ethel Marples of £1,000, matched by another £1,000 by Miss Marples' relatives, £2,000 raised by mortgage loan by the National Trust, and another £1,400 raised by the Executive Committee and other members of the Branch (within a fortnight).

VII

Rather than being a quiet interlude while attention was rightly focused elsewhere, the war years turned out to be just as busy for the Branch as the 1920s and 1930s. Such was the progress made, that by 1945 and the imminent end of the war in Europe at least, the Branch was not only the most experienced and influential local and regional conservation society in the country, but it was also poised, through Ethel's appointment in 1945 to the Hobhouse Committee, to make a national contribution.

But the war years took their toll in the deaths of a number of outstanding members of the organisation. The Annual Report for 1944 recorded the deaths of three outstanding members: F.W. Scorah, a founder member and member of the Executive Committee, who used his influence to interest Alderman Graves in the Blacka Moor campaign; Ethel Marples, whose bequest had contributed to the acquisition of Mam Tor and the Winnats; and Paul Crimp of the Royal Navy, whose photographs had been featured in the 1937 'Save the Countryside' exhibition and the *Housing in the Peak District* booklet. Finally, in December 1944, the death was announced of C. Douglas Yeomans, a pioneer member, and member of the Executive Committee, who undertook the raising of the fund for the Surprise View Appeal and was actively involved with the Longshaw Wardens.

5

Mingled hope and apprehension

1945–1951

I

AS THE WAR DREW TO AN END, there was general hope and anticipation in the country that a new era was dawning: after the unemployment of the thirties and six years of privation and suffering in the war, the British population looked forward to a future of reconstruction and a welfare state—a world of good housing, full employment and social security. Members of the Sheffield and Peak District Branch of the CPRE no doubt shared these general aspirations. More specifically, in the light of the Dower Report of April 1945 and the setting up of the Hobhouse Committee in July 1945 there must have been hopes among the Executive Committee and the general membership that a national park in the Peak District could be a reality in the foreseeable future. But there must also have been fears that reconstruction and post-war prosperity, if not controlled and guided by central, regional and local planning provisions and regulations, would bring with them an onslaught on the countryside to the west and south of Sheffield's built-up area, including the area proposed for a national park.

A return to peacetime also meant the demobilisation of Gerald, and by the beginning of 1946 he was back in post as Technical Secretary.

The early post-war years saw the death of three the Branch's most outstanding supporters. Professor Edward Forster, Chairman of the Branch from 1933 to 1948 and first Chairman of the Voluntary Joint Committee for the Peak District National Park, died in July 1950. He was succeeded as Chairman by the architect, Mr J. Mansell Jenkinson, who had been a member of the Executive for 20 years and Chairman of the Advisory Panel of Architects. The Branch's president since 1938, Sir William Rothenstein, died in 1945. With his national reputation and his local ties, Sir William had been, as the 1945 Annual Report aptly put, it 'an ideal president'. He was succeeded by

Lord Chorley of Kendal, Secretary of the CPRE. The Branch also suffered a great loss by the death in 1947 of their powerful ally, John Dower, at the early age of 46. Following his influential White Paper on National Parks in England and Wales in 1945, he had worked, with his health already failing, on the Hobhouse Committee, and continued to contribute to the Committee's work from his sick bed until the publication of the Hobhouse Report. In her script for a lantern talk in 1954, Ethel stated that when John Dower died, 'the main inspiration in the Government died too'.

Professor Edward Forster, chairman, 1933-48. He was also chairman of the Voluntary Joint Committee for the Peak District National Park from 1938 until 1947.

II

The major focus of both the Branch and the Voluntary Joint Committee in the immediate post-war years was the hoped-for designation of a national park in the Peak District—what was referred to in the Annual Report for 1951 as the Branch's 'grand purpose'. At the beginning of the period there was considerable basis for optimism: much of the spadework had been done in terms of setting up the Voluntary Joint Committee and mapping appropriate boundaries; the Dower Report was very supportive; the Government had set up the Hobhouse Committee; and Ethel was a member of that committee. But it was not likely to be all plain sailing: there was likely to be opposition from landowners, farmers and mineral interests; and local rivalries were likely to be resurrected when the tricky matter of administering a park straddling not only local district boundaries but also county boundaries was embarked upon. Then there was the matter of representation on the national park planning boards and committees. All these issues would no doubt lead to further wrangling and possible delays.

The Hobhouse Report was published in July 1947 and an area of 572 square miles in the Peak District was one of the four national parks included in the proposed first round of designations. The proposed boundaries (with Dovedale) of the Peak Park did not differ materially from those suggested

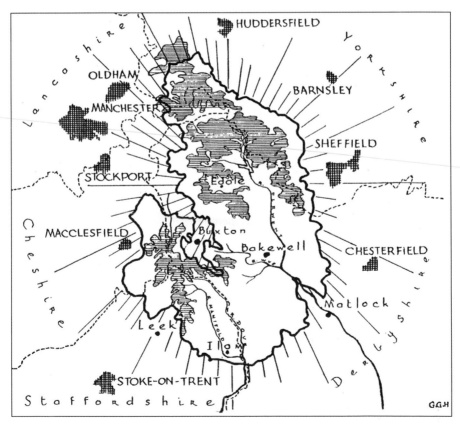

Boundaries of the Peak District National Park as proposed by the Hobhouse Committee. The map was drawn by Gerald and was used as the cover of the Annual Report from 1947 to 1950.

by the Voluntary Joint Committee. The Hobhouse Committee proposed that there should be a central authority, the National Parks Commission, and that each park should having its own planning board consisting of a Chairman appointed by the Commission, and with one half of the board's membership being appointed by the counties or county boroughs whose administrative areas fell wholly or partly within a park's boundaries, and the other half, drawn from the locality of the park in question, appointed by the Commission.

The National Parks Bill was eventually published in March 1948 but in the view of the Branch and the Voluntary Joint Committee it was unsatisfactory in a number of areas. First, it was proposed that the National Parks Commission would be an advisory body only, without executive powers or control of finance for national park purposes, as advocated in the Hobhouse Report. Secondly, the Bill proposed, again against the advice of the Hobhouse Committee, that three-quarters of the members of park planning authorities should be appointed by county and county borough councils, and the rest also elected by these councils, though nominated by the Ministry of Town and Country Planning. Thirdly, although the Bill gave powers to appoint a joint planning authority where parks covered the area of more than one local authority, there was an escape clause which permitted the Minister of Town and Country Planning to sanction only a joint advisory committee if the local authorities concerned could not agree to work together. This again went against the generally recognised common sense recommendation of Hobhouse that there should in every case be one planning authority for each park. The Branch's Annual Report for 1950 said 'there could hardly be a better means of ensuring the failure of a National Park from its outset'.

In the period immediately prior to the publication of the Hobhouse Report in July 1947 and the final passage of the National Parks Act in late 1949, certain interests let it be known that they opposed the establishment of a national park in the Peak District. It was reported at the Executive Meeting of the Branch at the end of March 1947 that 'a formidable opposition' had shown itself in the correspondence columns of the *High Peak News*, instigated, it was believed, by mineral interests. One opponent who was opposed to landscape preservation if it involved controlling quarrying or private building had announced that he was calling a public meeting in Bakewell Town Hall, but Ethel persuaded him to wait until the publication of the Hobhouse Report. Other opponents were members of the farming community, especially those in the Hope Valley who suffered greatly from trespass and vandalism. Gerald drafted a 'Countryside Code' in 1948, which was sent to NFU branches in the Peak, but the farmers and their representatives refused to co-operate. By late 1949 relations had improved and a joint committee, made up of members of the Derbyshire Hill Farmers' organisation and the Voluntary Joint Committee, was formed which put forward ways of combating bad behaviour through a combination of educational films and appropriate action by the police and magistrates. In April 1950 the NFU and educational, youth club, church and CPRE representatives met in Sheffield to plan other initiatives to curb vandalism in the Peak District by young visitors from Sheffield.

The National Parks and Access to the Countryside Act received Royal Assent in December 1949 but right up to the designation order for the Peak District National Park in December 1950, Derbyshire County Council opposed the idea of a joint board for the Peak District and persuaded the County Councils of Staffordshire, Cheshire, and the West Riding to join them in opposition. But Sheffield City Council supported the idea of a single planning board. The Voluntary Joint Committee lobbied ceaselessly through Parliament, the Ministry of Town and Country Planning, the National Parks Commission and in the press for a joint planning board and in the end the Minister, Hugh Dalton, gave in.

In June 1950, as a mark of its pioneering work, the Voluntary Joint Committee was sent by the National Parks Commission a draft map of the proposed Peak District National Park boundaries, with a request for comments within one month. The statutory obligation was to consult only with local authorities but the Chairman of the Commission, Sir Patrick Duff, felt that in the case of the Peak District he would like Ethel to be aware of the proposals at an early stage. Although the boundaries, in the main, followed the recommendations of the Hobhouse Committee, which in turn closely followed those recommended by the Voluntary Joint Committee, there were, in the view of the Joint Committee, some serious omissions. The Committee decided to make representations objecting to the omissions in two categories: first those areas which in the view of the Committee, it was essential to include within the proposed park boundaries, and secondly, those areas which should preferably be included in the park. The first list included Great Low near Hurdlow Town; the Upper Dove Valley (presented to the National Trust by F.A. Holmes); the whole of Woo Dale with its surrounding skyline; the crest of Bee Low; and the hill country north and south of Darley Dale comprising Gladwins Mark and Farley Moor, commanding a superb view of the Derwent Valley. The second list included land west of Barmoor Clough; Black Hill south of Disley; land east and south of Hayfield; Pott Shrigley and Nab Head; Gawsworth Common and Bosley Minn; the Bradbourne area; Onseacre; and land in the neighbourhood of Midhope. The areas were subsequently inspected by a member of the National Parks Commission in the company of Ethel and Gerald, but no changes were made. At the public inquiry held in Buxton in March 1951, Gerald put the case again for the inclusion of these areas, but representatives of the Voluntary Joint Committee were told that if they continued to press the claims for their inclusion it would mean the re-opening of the inquiry and probable delay in designating the Peak District as a national park. Faced with this predicament, the claims were withdrawn.

The designation order for the creation of a national park in the Peak District was eventually published in December 1950 and the Peak District National Park became a reality in April 1951. Sir Patrick Duff wrote to Ethel and Gerald informing them in advance of the event in view of their 'long and manful fight', which he hoped would continue.

III

And that fight would have to continue if proposed developments in the Peak District during the first six post-war years were any yardstick. At the National Park public inquiry at Buxton in 1951 Gerald had submitted a map of the proposed national park area showing 54 separate places where campaigns had been mounted since 1945 against developments threatening the scenery of the Peak District. Of these, opposition to the extension of limestone quarrying and cement production had been most time-consuming and ultimately least successful.

There were some successful campaigns. In October 1949, following a public inquiry at Bakewell in June 1948, the Minister of Town and Country Planning announced that he intended to refuse the application by Eyam Quarries Ltd. to open a quarry at Hammerton Hill, on the grounds that the natural beauty of Tideswell Dale would be seriously damaged. In November 1950 a public inquiry was held at Cheadle in connection with I.C.I.'s application to extend their Tunstead Quarry, then the largest in the United Kingdom. Gerald represented the Branch and the Voluntary Joint Committee and urged the preservation of the southern most tip of the escarpment between Woo Dale and Great Rocks Dale, and the planting of a screen of trees. The company agreed to both stipulations.

Hammerton Hill where an application to open a limestone quarry in 1948 was refused in 1949 following a public enquiry.

However, the decision by the Minister of Planning in March 1945 to grant permission to Earle's to establish a new cement works at Caldon Low on the southern boundary of the proposed Peak District National Park, following a public inquiry in November 1944, proved to be the first of a number of hammerblows to the Branch and to the Voluntary Joint Committee in their fight to prevent the expansion of limestone quarrying, clay and shale extraction, and cement manufacturing plants in the Peak District.

The Caldon Low decision was followed in November 1948, after a local inquiry at Buxton in February, by the decision to allow Derbyshire Stone Ltd. to break through the fine rock face which until that time had screened their workings from Ashwood Dale. The area in question was just 200 yards outside the proposed national park boundary.

The biggest blow came early in 1949 following the two-day public inquiry in April 1948 at Chapel-en-le Frith to consider proposals for expansion at the Hope Valley Cement Works. The company was requesting permission to increase its capacity by 40 per cent. The main proposals

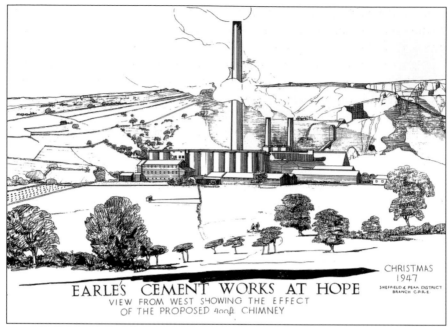

EARLE'S CEMENT WORKS AT HOPE
VIEW FROM WEST SHOWING THE EFFECT
OF THE PROPOSED 400ft CHIMNEY

CHRISTMAS 1947
SHEFFIELD & PEAK DISTRICT BRANCH C.P.R.E.

Drawing produced during the 1948 campaign against expansion at the Hope Valley Cement Works to show the effect of the proposed 400 feet high chimney. The two existing chimneys were 150 feet high.

were: the erection of a fifth kiln; the erection of a new chimney 400 feet high (250 feet higher than the existing chimneys); the extension of the limestone reserve to last 150 years; and the extension of clay workings into Marsh Farm on the Hope-Castleton road and Brough Farm on the unspoilt slopes of Bradwell Edge. The local authorities did not oppose the application and the Peak Joint Planning Committee was satisfied to demand concessions. Both were swayed by employment considerations. Opposition to the proposal was presented by Ethel on behalf of the Branch and the National Trust and by Gerald on behalf of the Voluntary Joint Committee. Twelve other local amenity societies also gave evidence. The case for the opposition argued that, first, as the firm had already confirmed that it had sufficient materials for twenty years, there should be a review at the end of that term not now; secondly, that the works at Caldon Low, just outside the proposed national park boundary, sanctioned in 1945 but not yet started, should be established; and thirdly, that instead of a large chimney, an efficient precipitator should be installed to get rid of the dust nuisance. At the outset the promoters made one concession: they would only ask for a limestone quarry life of 117 years instead of 150. This concession, which was in response to a request from the Voluntary Joint Committee, meant that there would be a barrier between the extended quarries and Pindale. In the event, in January 1949, the Minister of Town and Country Planning gave the promoters everything they had asked for. A government elected on the platform of full employment was not swayed by conservation considerations. The decision was followed by public indignation, protests by MPs and letters in the press, most notably one to the *Manchester Guardian* signed by the Bishops of Derby, Manchester and Sheffield, and one to *The Times* signed by Lord Crawford, Chairman of the National Trust, Sir Patrick Abercrombie, Chairman of the CPRE, and Sir Norman Birkett, Chairman of the Standing Committee on National Parks. Subsequently the Branch published an illustrated small leaflet entitled *The Hope Valley Disaster.* Its sub-title was 'Is it common sense to create an industrial zone in the heart of a national park?'

The new chimney at the Hope Valley Cement Works. The photograph appeared in the 1951 Annual Report.

to Parliament by the National Trust, the National Farmers' Union and local amenity societies, principally the North Staffordshire Field Club. In May 1946 a Select Committee of the House of Lords rejected the Bill. The reasons for rejecting the Bill were not published but were thought to be a combination of serious doubt about the geological suitability of the valley based on the evidence provided by the Voluntary Joint Committee's consultant geologist, Edgar Morton; the possibility of using other water sources; and a claim by the South Staffordshire Water Company to a share in the control and use of the impounded waters.

Land in the Peak District was also coveted by the Government for military purposes. In late 1945 Leash Fen and the Burbage Valley were briefly used for ammunition disposal but the activity stopped, with an apology from the Army's Northern Command after representations from the Executive Committee. However, in early 1947 it became known that the War Department wished to use 1,500 acres in the Burbage Valley as a Territorial Training Ground. Despite protests from the Executive Committee, local ramblers' groups and the YHA, and a letter to the *Sheffield Telegraph*, the City Council approved the use of the area, under certain conditions, for military training. The Executive Committee responded by sending a letter on behalf of all local protesters to the Services Land Requirements Committee suggesting alternative sites and asking for a public inquiry. By the autumn of 1946 the Army had withdrawn its proposals. Almost immediately the Ministry of Defence indicated that it wished to use 3,400 acres within the boundaries of the proposed Peak District National Park, north-west of Upper Hulme, Staffordshire, for a training area including a mortar range. This proposal, thankfully, was quietly dropped.

An increasing problem in the immediate post-war years was the pro-liferation in the countryside of caravans, shacks and other temporary dwellings. The worst increase was in Sheffield's Green Belt, especially in the Dore Moor area, but it was also a problem within the boundaries of the proposed national park. This was particularly common at weekends when mobile canteens appeared at popular bus stops such as Fox House. In the case of caravan dwellings, the local authorities were accused of not applying the maximum legal period rule (28 days) with strictness and uniformity.

There was also concern about ribbon development. The 1947 Annual Report mentioned the siting of prefabricated houses at Hope which had increased this phenomenon. Other examples cited were around Calver Sough crossroads and between Curbar and Froggatt. The 1950 Annual Report also commented on the tendency towards geometrically planned layouts, instead of 'four-square compactness' with village streets.

The Town and Country Planning Act of 1947, if 'wisely enacted', was seen by the Executive Committee to be a major new force for ensuring suitable development in rural areas. It came into force on 1 July 1948 and for the first time planning was placed entirely in the control of County and County Borough Councils. Development Plans were required under the Act within three years. A major cause of regret was that the new act meant that the Peak Joint Planning Committee, which since its inception in 1935, had been a major influence in limiting defacement and encouraging appropriate development, would cease to exist.

The work of the voluntary Advisory Panel of Architects, moth-balled during the war years, began to operate again with the return of Gerald from the Forces and the Annual Report for 1946 reported that local quarry owners and stone merchants had been circularised about the availability and prices of local stone with a view to encouraging its use when house building increased. Throughout the second half of the 1940s the Branch Annual Reports reported on raised standards of new housing in the Peak District with 'a cheering amount of new building in stone and with a certain local feeling in design' as the 1949 Annual Report put it. To encourage further the use of stone in the Peak District, a new committee—The Peak District Stone Committee—was set up in 1950, under the chairmanship of the Branch Chairman, Mansell Jenkinson, with Gerald as Secretary.

In 1948 it was announced that it was proposed to drive a new tunnel through the Pennines at Woodhead as part of the scheme to electrify the line. At a meeting with representatives of the Railway Executive, the Ministry of Town and Country Planning and the West Riding Council, held at Dunford Bridge in June 1948, the Railway Executive agreed to the Branch's suggestions, put by Gerald, that the top soil should be saved to cover the spoil from the tunnel, the spoil to be 'contoured' and planted with native trees. They further agreed that the tunnel entrances and the new station at Dunford Bridge would be of local stone or reconstructed stone blocks.

In June 1949 information reached the Branch that the BBC intended to build a television transmitter station at an elevation of 1,700 feet on Holme Moss, south-west of Holmfirth, within the boundaries of the proposed Peak District National Park. The mast would be 750 feet high and visible for many miles around. A site meeting was arranged between Gerald, Fred Marshall, MP, and the civil engineer and architect of the BBC. Although no concession was made about the site, the BBC agreed to construct the station buildings in stone and the curtilage wall also in stone, dry laid. The request that the roofs should be pitched not flat, was refused on technical grounds.

An account of activity in the immediate post-war years would be incomplete without reference to the severe winter of 1946–47 which brought an unexpected call on the Branch's resources and organisational expertise and which also provided widespread publicity for the cause. The Derbyshire War Agricultural Committee telephoned Endcliffe Vale House one Friday in February 1947 to ask if the Secretaries could get in touch with ramblers and others who knew the moors well, who might help to save 400 starving sheep on Stanage Moors. Gerald managed to organise a party of 60 who turned up at Hathersage station on the Sunday morning. The party carried sacks of hay, often through waist-high drifts to the flocks on Bole Hill. Over the next two weekends, larger volunteer parties were organised— over 200 people in all on each occasion—made up of ramblers from Sheffield and Chesterfield, members of the Youth Hostels Association, Holiday Fellowship, Co-operative Holidays Association and many other individual volunteers, who rescued and fed sheep on Big Moor, Totley Moss and the Derwent Moors and searched for a missing farmer at Bradfield. The RSPCA sent officers, Sheffield Transport Department laid on extra buses and the *Sheffield Telegraph* and *The Star* publicised the venture. Altogether some 1,500 sheep were fed.

Sheep rescue party, Froggatt Edge, February 1947. Gerald is on the left.

V

Continual vigilance was not only the watchword in the case of the area covered by the proposed Peak District National Park: it was also the guiding principle in the battle to protect Sheffield's provisional Green Belt. In the light of the successful campaign against residential development on the Fulwood Hall estate in 1944, it was decided at the Executive Meeting in January 1945 to form a special sub-committee of 'Watchers' whose business it would be to watch the Green Belt and assist the Executive Committee to act when occasion required. The sub-committee was to have no executive powers and would simply report to the Executive Committee. It was decided to restrict the membership to no more than twenty and to invite Mr J.P. Ardron to join the Executive Committee and to lead the new group. The Green Belt Sub-Committee held its first meeting on 27 March 1945, with not only CPRE Branch members but also representatives from other local societies.

The major event in 1945 in connection with the Sheffield Green Belt was the publication in February of *Sheffield's Green Belt*, a booklet written on behalf of the Branch by Wallace Hunt and illustrated with more than twenty photographs (mostly by the author), many with long captions. The publication emphasised the almost unique position of Sheffield in not being hemmed in by other industrial towns and cities, and the unique opportunity it was afforded to create a continuous green belt in the west and south, if not in the north and east. It went on to praise the acquisition of land in the proposed green belt by the City Council (the most recent being the purchase in July 1944 of the Totley Hall estate, comprising the hall itself and 160 acres of farmland and woodland) and by benefactors such as Alderman Graves and Mr T. Walter Hall.

The main point of the publication was, however, to sound a warning note in a section entitled 'Danger Ahead'. The main message in this section was that although there had already been outstanding successes there was still an element of uncertainty. Would the City Council make sure that the line was held against applications for permission for piece-meal and unco-ordinated development? The points were made that the surviving farms were of the minimum working size and further loss of land would make efficient farming impossible, and that incremental small-scale development would inexorably destroy the 'wholeness' of the green belt scenery. Anticipating the post-war demand for housing in the urban fringe, there was an urgent plea for the exact boundaries of the Green Belt to be fixed and all applications for incursions beyond that boundary to be resisted 'whatever pressure may be brought to bear'. 'Now is the moment', was the conclusion, 'when the resolution of those responsible for seeing the scheme through is likely to be put to the test'.

Within two months 4,000 copies of the first edition of 5,000 copies of *Sheffield's Green Belt* had been disposed of and a reprint of a further 4,000 ordered.

In August 1945 a public inquiry took place at Sheffield Town Hall in connection with an application to develop a housing estate in three fields on Mooredge Farm, Totley, north of the Totley–Owler Bar Road within the Green Belt. The City Council had refused permission and the owner of the land had appealed against the decision. The City Council's stand was supported by fifteen organisations including the CPRE whose case was stated by Executive Committee member Arthur Irons. In dismissing the appeal, the Minister for Town and Country Planning said he was satisfied that the proposed development 'would seriously prejudice the general character of the surrounding area of great value to Sheffield as a whole'.

In 1948 the British Electricity Authority proposed to supply high tension power from Staythorpe to Oughtibridge and proposed to do this by erecting pylons round the west of the city, which would cause serious disfigurement in the Green Belt. This was vigorously opposed through strongly worded resolutions to the City Council, neighbouring local authorities and to the Ministry of Town and Country Planning. A shorter route round the east of the city, where much less harm would be done to landscape quality was proposed. By January 1949 Gerald was able to report to the Executive Committee that the western route seemed to have been abandoned.

A threat to the Green Belt came in 1949 from a most unusual quarter—the Education Committee. Under the 1944 Education Act new secondary schools were required, and with the post-war 'baby boom' new primary schools were also needed. A twenty-year plan envisaged that 175 new schools would be built in Sheffield including a number in the Green Belt at Greenhill Moor, Hallam Grange, Norton, Ringinglow, Totley Bents, Rivelin Valley, Whirlow, and Wyming Brook. One of the earliest cases was the Maud Maxwell School at Ringinglow where the Branch's protestations about the location, the specific site and choice of materials were all ignored. Even more worrying was the use of Totley Hall, the finest old building in the Green Belt, as a Teachers' Training College. Extensions were being considered in 1949 and as the Annual Report for that year put it: 'it is, of course, of the utmost importance that these should, both in design and materials, be worthy of the existing 17th century building.' In the event the old hall was surrounded by modern extensions, some faced in stone after representations by the Branch and the Society for the Protection of Ancient Buildings, but also including the concrete and glass multi-storey Lowfield Building which was demolished in 1999.

In 1950 it was reported that Sheffield Corporation proposed to build an estate of approximately 7,000 houses south of Greenhill as far as the city boundary. Dronfield Urban District Council was strongly opposed to the proposal, fearing that in the future there could be encroachment across the city boundary into the 'rural reserve' between Sheffield and Dronfield. The Executive Committee, although deciding it could not oppose the proposal because the area lay outside the Sheffield Green Belt, decided the Branch should be represented at the public inquiry to register opposition to cross-boundary encroachment and to try to endeavour to obtain a guarantee that it would not occur.

The immediate post-war period ended on a very disquieting note. Sheffield City Council submitted to Parliament the Sheffield Extension Bill which proposed acquiring 1,400 acres from Derbyshire and 6,490 acres from the West Riding for housing development. The proposed expansion into the West Riding would result in the urbanisation of the Loxley Valley and the spread of the city in the Bradfield area up to the borders of the Peak District National Park. The Bill was rejected by the House of Lords in the summer of 1951. This was a cause for celebration but also for concern. Rejection of the Extension Bill meant that attention might be turned to land within the city boundaries in the provisional Green Belt.

VI

In 1944 the Branch had lobbied successfully for a postponement of open-cast coal mining activity at Bowden Housteads Wood in Sheffield. Subsequently, nearly fourteen acres were lost. This proved to be only one of a number of campaigns to prevent the desecration of the remaining pockets of attractive countryside in the coalfield districts in South Yorkshire and North Derbyshire and at Lyme Handley and the Three Shires Head area in the proposed Peak District National Park.

There were some outstanding successes. In May 1950, a petition, organised by Gerald, and signed by 7,600 supporters within a week, was sent to the Prime Minister, objecting to the proposed open-casting on Hazlehurst Farm and Delves Wood in the Moss valley, an area bought by Sheffield Corporation in 1939 to protect that part of the southern approaches to Sheffield. In August the Branch was informed by the Ministry of Fuel and Power that 'they were not proposing to undertake any work...because the

The Cordwell Valley, threatened by open-cast coal mining operations in 1950.

Open-cast mining at Wentworth.

estimated cost would result in a financial loss which…would not be justifiable'. But within weeks it became known that open-cast mining was being contemplated in the Cordwell Valley, with boring taking place on four farms: Barlow Woodseats Hall, Johnnygate, Cowley Hall and Barlow Highfields. Objections were even more vociferous than in the case of the Moss Valley proposal against the desecration of this ancient agricultural landscape of ancient halls, woodlands and hedged fields, what the 1951 Annual Report called an area of 'ancient and homely beauty'. Protests were made to the Minister of Fuel and Power by Sheffield, Chesterfield and Derbyshire local authorities, by ten local societies and nine local MPs. In February 1951, the Minister, Philip Noel Baker, received direct representations from the CPRE and gave assurances that the Cordwell Valley would not be disturbed.

Local protests, supported by the Branch even though the site was outside its area of responsibility at that time, were, however, to no avail in the case of the most notorious open-cast scheme—that on Earl Fitzwilliam's Wentworth Woodhouse estate between Barnsley and Rotherham. Open-cast operations had begun there as early as 1943 and were to continue until the early 1950s. Large areas of farmland were lost, including the whole area between Hague Lane and the Sheffield-Barnsley road (A6135) in the western half of the township. Mining operations, which had previously come to within yards of the great terrace wall bounding the southern edge of the gardens, then took place within the gardens themselves, almost reaching the front door of the westward-facing Baroque frontage. These operations took place against a background of outrage and protest supported by the vast majority of the local population who saw the park and estate landscape at Wentworth as one of the last remaining islands of historic countryside in the area. In a report in the *Sheffield Telegraph* as early as 1945, a First World War veteran said the landscape reminded him of '1917 and the scenery around Paschendaele'. At one point local coal miners even contemplated strike action. To many observers the open-cast operations at Wentworth looked like a personal vendetta by Emanuel Shinwell, the Minister of Fuel and Power, against Earl Fitzwilliam, a representative of the old order. By the beginning of the 1950s, half of Wentworth township had been turned upside down. As early as 1947, the Annual Report for that year described a countryside already almost entirely stripped of its former character:

> *The present appearance of Wentworth…is even worse than was imagined when intense public effort was made to save the famous house and park last year. The well-wooded, well-*

farmed area, which also served as an open space for an industrial population, is now a scene of desolation. Some agricultural land has been restored, but not satisfactorily, according to farmers. In any case its charm is entirely lost. Instead of hedges, peaceful lanes and sheltering woods, is a monotonous plain with concrete roads and fences, which none would visit for pleasure.

VII

Complaints about unsightly, and in some cases unnecessary, lopping of street trees in Sheffield, particularly in the older western suburbs, which had been the subject of representations to the City Council in the second half of the 1930s, flared up again in 1945. The 1946 Annual Report referred to this as a 'holocaust, when graceful forest trees—perhaps Sheffield's only remaining beauty—were reduced to mutilated stumps, regardless of their natural species or shape'. Representations were again made to the City Council's Highways Committee but without success.

More lopping went on in the winter of 1945–46 and it was reported that public protest was more marked than ever. At that point the Branch thought it would be useful to obtain the advice of an expert. Accordingly, Mr A.D.C. Le Sueur, consultant forester to the City of London, was employed in August 1946 to inspect the city's trees and draw up a report. While recognising the difficult problems facing local authorities, he concluded that in Sheffield ' pruning appears to be worked on a general plan to all species, without regard to the fact that different species react differently. Trees have been lopped for no apparent reason.' He recommended that a full-time arboriculturist should be employed as in Birmingham and Liverpool.

The Executive Committee concluded that there was no hope of improvement until an expert was appointed and in the interim they decided to raise public awareness and that of those in authority by issuing 4,000 copies of a small leaflet written by Gerald entitled *Town Trees* which was published in October 1947. Well illustrated with examples of both crude and unnecessary lopping and of mature trees forming a background to and a foil to architectural features, the booklet gave advice on doing a necessary preliminary survey, pruning obstructive and unhealthy trees, repairing and prolonging the life of old trees, felling and replanting. Emphasis was placed on the modern practice of progressive pruning over a number of years

Unsightly lopping of roadside trees, Fulwood Road, Sheffield.

rather than the Sheffield practice of heavy pruning at long intervals. The booklet was well reviewed in the press, eliciting leading articles in the *Manchester Guardian* and the *Sheffield Telegraph* and a column in the *Observer*. Subsequently, constructive meetings were held with Council officials about the treatment of the city's trees.

Timber shortages and high prices in the late 1940s also led to tree felling in the Peak District. The removal of all the beeches in Cranside Wood on the north side of the Wye between Cressbrook Mill and Litton Mill in the winter of 1948–49 and of riverside trees below Thornhill on an attractive stretch of the River Derwent, caused the Branch to urge local planning authorities to take advantage of their powers to make tree preservation orders. The absence of such an order meant that Whaley Bridge Rural

District Council declared itself powerless to prevent the felling of the avenue of beeches known as the Taxal Beeches in the autumn of 1948. Local residents started a Taxal Beeches Fund to which the Branch subscribed and £275 was raised to prevent the felling. Subsequently, Derbyshire County Council made comprehensive preservation orders for groups of trees in the Wye and Derwent valleys.

Members of the Hobhouse Committee on a site survey visit. Ethel is on the left, and the figure in the middle is John Dower.

VIII

The setting up of the Peak District as the first national park, the maintenance of the integrity of the Sheffield Green Belt (just), the incessant battle
against disfigurement within the Park and elsewhere, often accompanied
by the preparation and presentation of evidence at public inquiries, meant
an energy-sapping routine for members of the Executive Committee,
especially for Ethel and Gerald, in the immediate post-war years. For Ethel,
with her work on the Hobhouse Committee as well as for the Branch and
the Voluntary Joint Committee this must have been particularly so. Her
work on the Hobhouse Committee alone, involved, over a two-year period,
80 meetings in London and seventeen site surveys of prospective national
park locations. She later described the Hobhouse Committee work as
'gruelling'.

But there was also public recognition. The period saw the conferment
of two major honours on Ethel for her unstinting work in the cause of
countryside preservation over a quarter of a century. In 1947 she was
awarded the MBE, one of the first awards for countryside conservation
activity for the voluntary sector. Among the more than fifty surviving
letters and telegrams of congratulation, a number quite bluntly state that
she and the cause which she had led for so long deserved a higher award.
Then in 1951 she was awarded the honorary degree of Master of Arts by
the University of Sheffield. In his speech on the conferment of the MA,
the Public Orator, Professor Dennis Browne, dubbed Ethel 'a sleepless
guardian' of the beauty of the countryside. ' Such devoted, unselfish and
successful endeavour', he went on, 'must command from a University the
deepest admiration and sympathy'.

The designation of the Peak District as the first national park in England
and Wales was, of course, the jewel in the crown of the Branch's
achievements, but the event was viewed, with a realism borne of many
other long drawn-out campaigns, like the continuing one of the Sheffield
Green Belt, only as a partial, provisional victory. The future of the Park
was still problematic and, like the whole of the immediate post-war period,
was one of 'mingled hope and apprehension' as the 1946 Annual Report
had put it. Five years later, the Annual Report for 1950 offered gratitude
and congratulations to the National Parks Commission but privately there
was disappointment that the Commission was headed by a retired civil
servant with no record of interest in the countryside, and that the
commissioners included not one member of the Hobhouse Committee.
There was also disappointment about the make-up of the Peak Park Joint
Planning Board. Not only were non-political representatives restricted to

Ethel, 'sleepless guardian of the beauty of the countryside', receiving her honorary MA at the University of Sheffield in 1951.

one-third of the membership, but only one member of the Branch—Gerald —and only one other member of the Voluntary Joint Committee had been appointed to the Board. The omission of others who had helped create the Park, from a share of its management, was 'a cause of bewilderment' in the words of the 1952 Annual Report. There survive in the Branch Archive two lists drawn up in 1950 by the Voluntary Joint Committee, at the request of the Standing Committee on National Parks for submission to the National Parks Commission, of persons recommended for consideration for non-political appointment to the Peak Park Joint Planning Board. Each recommendation is supported by a potted biography emphasising countryside conservation/planning experience. The first draft is in alphabetical order. The Standing Committee then asked for the list to be in order of priority. There is a list A (eight names) and a list B (seven names). Ethel was number one on list A. She was not appointed. The two successful candidates, Gerald and D.W.F. Shilton (Secretary of the Co-operative Holidays Association and a member of the Standing Committee on National Parks) were numbers two and five on list A. Three of the other five non-political appointees subsequently named as members of the Board were unknown to members of the Voluntary Joint Committee.

The 1950 Annual Report, reflecting all these disappointments, summed up the situation thus:

> *The question now is: Will it be a genuine National Park or only so in name? If the park is considered a priority for major industrial ventures, for indiscriminate scattering of villas, cafés and caravans, rather than a region whose natural beauty is the dominant concern, where true rural prosperity, farming, woods and wild life are encouraged, our labours will have been in vain.*

6

Short-term expediency vs the permanent good

1952–1960

I

THE GENERAL ELECTION in the autumn of 1951 heralded a decade or so of economic growth and the emergence of the affluent society echoed by Harold Macmillan's 1957 claim that 'you've never had it so good'. It also unleashed a period of unrelenting pressure to develop in the countryside: housing in particular, but also roads and industry. And whereas the Labour Government between 1945 and 1951 had not always found it to be in its own interests to stop developments because of its commitment to full employment and a large-scale housing programme, successive Conservative governments throughout the 1950s found their planning policies had to bow to free enterprise and business as well as a general expectation that the main features of the post-war welfare state would continue.

Looking back on the 1950s, the Annual Report for 1961 sounded a warning note about prevailing attitudes:

> *The difficulties which confront all who realise the value of Rural England and the need for sound national planning have increased in the past ten years; ever since the vital impetus which led to the creation of new towns and national parks has been permitted to subside: but the resultant confusion and deterioration of the face of our land is only now becoming generally apparent.*
>
> *The siting of nuclear power stations in our noblest scenery; the countenancing in some instances of expansion into Green Belts of cities already overblown, in fact of allowing expediency to prevail over permanent good, make the task of establishing*

a seemly background for living extremely hard. The pressure comes not only from defence requirements and financial ebullience, but from the unexpected increase of population and its need for better living conditions. Yet these include fresh food and contact with nature. A nation of town dwellers would be anaemic in body and soul.

The report went on:

The core of the Peak, beneficently controlled by the Peak Park authority, is for that reason protected in the main: but on the outskirts of each neighbouring town, the gentler landscape of wood and farmland, which should be a source of delight to every citizen, is more often than not subject to outrage. This is due to inadequate planning and still more to ignorance of architectural fundamentals.

Combating assaults on the local countryside around Sheffield and in the Peak Park meant a succession of public inquiries which imposed not only a financial burden on the Branch in providing the services of counsel, which had to be met by a long series of requests to members for support for fighting funds, but also an unremitting schedule of preparing cases and briefing counsel, a burden that fell on the shoulders of Ethel and Gerald. Gerald had the additional task of appearing as expert witness at most of the public inquiries.

In the middle of the decade, in October 1956, Mrs T.W. Ward died. This meant that Endcliffe Vale House, which Mrs Ward had generously made available as the Branch headquarters since 1924, had to be sold, and new Branch offices had to be found. The last Executive Committee meeting took place at Endcliffe Vale House on 26 November 1956, and the first at 22 Endcliffe Crescent, Gerald and Ethel's new home, on 28 May 1957.

II

Whereas in the immediate post-war years the main focus of attention of the Executive Committee had been the creation of the Peak District National Park and the fight against the expansion of the quarrying and cement making industries there, the 1950s were to prove to be centred much more on a series of campaigns to attempt to maintain Sheffield's Green Belt. And the main adversary was not the private developer but Sheffield City Council.

The last Executive Committee meeting at Endcliffe Vale House, 26 November 1956.   At the head of the table are Ethel (on the left), J. Mansell Jenkinson (Chairman, centre) and Gerald (right).

LAST MOMENTS AT E.V.H.

Cartoon by Gerald showing the 'last moments at Endcliffe Vale House'. The removals men are inconvenienced by Gertrude who can't leave the piano, Gerald completing his yoga exercise and Ethel pulling out her hair after reading that there is a Butlin's holiday camp on Kinder Scout.

The rejection by the House of Lords in 1951 of the Sheffield Extension Bill meant that Sheffield's housing needs in the short to medium term would have to be met from within the existing city boundaries and this meant that land in the provisional Green Belt was likely to come under threat. By February 1952 there were reports in the local press that the Town Planning Committee had proposed to the City Council that land in the Green Belt at five major locations should be used for housing: 217 acres in the Meersbrook Valley and at Gleadless; 42 acres at Stannington overlooking the Rivelin Valley; 50 acres at Bradway (together with nearly another 90 acres across the city boundary in Derbyshire); 88 acres at Totley south of Totley Old Hall; and 34 acres at Fox Hill to the east of Back Edge.

The Executive Committee asked the Town Planning, Estates and Housing Committees and the appropriate Council officers to receive a deputation from the Branch before the next meeting of the City Council on 5 March. This took place on 1 March and consisted of the Chairman, the two Secretaries, the Bishop of Sheffield, and six members of the Executive Committee including Fred Marshall and G.H.B Ward. In objecting to the proposals, Gerald, who put the case for the CPRE, made four main points: blitzed and cleared areas in the inner city should be used for housing development before farmland on the periphery was sacrificed; other land outside the inner city not in the Green Belt at Handsworth, Greenhill, Arbourthorne, Hackenthorpe and Brincliffe should be used; land should be conserved by building at higher densities and the use of flats; and that serious consideration should be given to the 19,000 overspill scheme in north-east Derbyshire recently put forward in the Derbyshire County Development Plan (and the subject of a report in *The Star* on 28 February 1952).

The deputation was cordially received but when the final version of the Development Plan was displayed in the Central Library from 29 March to 16 April, no concessions had been made. The most disquieting feature of the plan from the Branch's point of view was the failure to identify Green Belt land as such. In previous maps of Sheffield showing planning intentions, the Green Belt had been shown as a permanent agricultural reservation and allotted a specific notation. The 1952 Annual Report noted that 'This is now omitted and the public left to assume its existence, where the map is left uncoloured. It is to be hoped that this is merely a technical oversight.' In a letter to Gerald in September 1952, in response to the Branch's representations with regard to the Draft Development Plan (sent on 1 April 1952), the Town Clerk had responded by saying that the map accompanying the Development Plan had been drawn up in accordance with Ministry circulars which made no provision for a specific green belt notation.

A public inquiry, lasting four days, to consider the City Council's proposals to acquire land for housing purposes in the provisional Green Belt was opened in Sheffield Town Hall on 21 October 1952. The CPRE case, supported by a petition containing 6,565 signatures, was put by Arthur Irons who called upon ten witnesses including Gerald and Ethel; J. Mansell Jenkinson, Dr Edward Bramley and Fred Marshall from the Branch Executive Committee; and George Langley-Taylor, Vice-Chairman of the CPRE. Langley-Taylor had been specifically sent from London to the inquiry to lodge objections on behalf of the CPRE National Executive, whose chairman was Sir Patrick Abercrombie, formerly consultant town planner to Sheffield City Council. In his evidence Langley-Taylor reported that Sir Patrick 'strongly regretted the proposed reversal of policy', and knowing the city well 'considered the fine country which lies around the city as a feature that many other places would envy, and it is one that should be held on to at all costs'. Other interests objecting to the proposals included the Sheffield Ramblers, the Hallamshire Footpaths Society, the National Farmers' Union, Derbyshire County Council (which was concerned about suburban sprawl and offered to find 6,000 house sites near Mosbrough and Eckington), and Dronfield Rural District Council. In the final paragraph of her evidence, Ethel commented on the disappointment and dismay felt within the local branch of the CPRE at the reneging on Green Belt policy by the City Council:

> *Finally, may I express our regret that we are obliged in this instance to oppose the Corporation with whom in the course of 27 years' work we have been in constant contact and where we have many friends. There are very few instances of Public Inquiries where we have not been on the Corporation's side. It is incomprehensible that a city for fourteen years should have pursued a policy to preserve <u>for all time</u> its greatest natural assets, and suddenly to reverse this policy, disintegrate its plan and disillusion its inhabitants. Industrial cities are not pleasant places, but Sheffield has always been held unique in one respect—the quality of the countryside at its doors.*

The inquiry, according to the Minutes of the Executive Meeting of 1 December, was conducted in a good tempered way until the summing-up speech on behalf of the City Council by the Town Clerk, John Heys. Making the point that for the sake of the loss of $2^{1/2}$ per cent of the Green Belt, the 33,000 people on the Council's housing list would have to wait a further two years (on the basis that housing sites presently under development would be finished by the end of 1954 and it would be 1955 before building could begin on sites outside the city boundary), he pointed out that the membership of the local branch of the CPRE was under 1,200 out of a population of over 500,000. He then summed up the issue as 'The view for the few—or houses for the many'.

This incensed the members of the Executive Committee and he was accused of misrepresenting and reviling the CPRE. It was resolved to send a statement of protest to the Lord Mayor which he was asked to read at the next meeting of the City Council. The two substantive paragraphs in the statement were as follows:

> *We consider in particular that the imputation that our objections could be summed up as 'a view for the few—against houses for the many' was not only an unfair description of the careful and well documented case we presented, but calculated to harm our organisation which contains many distinguished citizens, and which has a long and honourable record of service to Sheffield, and also to the Corporation. This record shows beyond question that our objects have always been to benefit all the citizens of Sheffield, and not any particular section.*
>
> *It is hardly necessary to point out that the policy which the C.P.R.E. sought to defend at the Inquiry was the Corporation's own Green Belt policy, approved in 1938 and vigorously pursued up to the time of the sudden reversal of that policy in February last.*

The letter was read out in full by the Town Clerk himself at the City Council Meeting on 7 January 1953.

On 4 March 1953 the Minister gave an interim judgement on the public inquiry, stating that he had sought to hold the balance between, on the one hand, the pressing need for housing, and, on the other, that of food production and the green belt. First, he recommended that scattered sites throughout the city capable of carrying 1,700 houses should be developed. Secondly, he gave permission for the compulsory purchase of land in the Gleadless Valley for housing development without modification, provided that the hamlet of Hemsworth was not too closely encircled and that due attention was given to the appearance of new development from the lower part of the valley. Thirdly, he refused to allow development at Stannington overlooking the Rivelin Valley. Decisions on the Bradway, Totley and Back Edge proposals were deferred until a later date. In February 1954

The Totley area of the Green Belt.

the Minister gave his final verdict. He gave permission for 32 out of 34 acres at Back Edge to be compulsorily purchased for housing development; however, he only allowed permission for 55 out of the 138 acres applied for at Bradway; and in the case of the 88 acres requested south of Totley Old Hall, he did not allow any to be used for housing.

While the final verdict of the October 1952 public inquiry was being awaited, another public inquiry had to be prepared for, this time in connection with the Sheffield Development Plan which had been submitted for approval to the Minister in July 1952. The Development Plan inquiry took place in July 1953. Objections were again made against the incursions into the provisional Green Belt which had been the subject of the October 1952 public inquiry, but the main bone of contention was that no formal recognition of a green belt was included in the plan. All farmland hitherto included in the provisional Green Belt was left uncoloured with a note

'Agricultural areas are as on the Ordnance Map'. At the inquiry, the Town Planning Officer, Mr J.M. Collie, gave the assurance that the unshaded and un-notated areas of farmland were 'not to be interfered with and will exist as shown in the plan in their existing use'.

The Development Plan, with modifications, was not finally approved by the Minister until 1957, but while it was on his desk awaiting his attention another storm blew up in early 1954 over the City Council's decision to allow housing development to take place on twelve acres of land in the provisional Green Belt (i.e. unallocated land in the Development Plan) in Newfield Lane and Townhead Road at Dore. Much more seriously, it became known that the City Council had resolved to make a compulsory purchase order on a further 150 acres at Gleadless in addition to the 208 acres already sanctioned. This would necessitate another public inquiry. The Newfield Lane/Townhead Road decision prompted the Executive to ask the Secretaries to write to the Minister of Housing and Local Government to ask if this was legal. The gist of their enquiry was: if the City Council could change the provisions of the Development Plan without referring to the Minister, then what status, if any, did the Development Plan have ? Four times a letter was sent to the Minister but only printed acknowledgements of receipt were received. Then in June 1954 the Minister distributed Circular 45/54 entitled 'Town and Country Planning (Development Plans) Direction 1954'. The Circular authorised local authorities to grant permission for development which did not accord with their Development Plan, without prior reference to the Minister, provided that the proposal neither involved a substantial departure from the plan nor injuriously affected the amenity of adjoining land. However the circular did stipulate that proposals not in accordance with the plan affecting *white land* (i.e. Green Belt land) 'would require prior reference to the Minister'.

The controversy surrounding incursions into the Sheffield Green Belt prompted Gerald to write an article entitled 'A New Sheffield' which was published in *Town and Country Planning* in the summer of 1955 and subsequently distributed in booklet form. The main thrust of the article was that Sheffield seemed determined to house and re-house its population within its boundaries, either through extending those boundaries (already turned down by the House of Lords in 1951) or building in the provisional Green Belt. The general cause of this policy, argued Gerald, was pride in the size of the city and a desire not to lose rateable value to neighbouring authorities. The courageous and imaginative answer, Gerald concluded, was to develop a satellite new town—the New Sheffield of the title—not just over the city boundary where Derbyshire County Council had offered sites to accommodate 19,000 people in the Mosbrough-Eckington area, but further east, possibly in north Nottinghamshire or Lincolnshire. Here the New Sheffield would not be 'off the map' but near the Great North Road and the London–Edinburgh railway, where flat land would make airport construction easy, and where industry would not be at the competitive disadvantage complained about by many Sheffield firms.

Concern over incursions into the Green Belt within Sheffield's boundaries, and existing and proposed developments in the North Derbyshire and West Riding Green Belts resulted in the Executive Committee sending a deputation to Sheffield City Council's Town Planning Committee in February 1957. The deputation, through Gerald, expressed the opinion that the City Council had not recently 'held so firmly to the leadership in progressive Green Belt planning' and the deputation asked if, in accordance with the Ministry of Housing and Local Government's Circular 42/55, it was possible for a formal Green Belt scheme to be submitted early that year. It was further pointed out that most of the green belt land surrounding Sheffield was either in Derbyshire or in the West Riding (32,000 out of 36,000 acres), and that unsuitable development was being allowed by the Derbyshire and West Riding County Councils, citing recent examples at Holmesfield in Derbyshire and Stannington in the West Riding. A joint green belt scheme with the two neighbouring authorities, was strongly urged, as quickly as possible. The point was also made strongly, on the lines of Gerald's argument in his *Town and Country Planning* article of 1955, that the establishment of a satellite town some distance from the city was the only practical solution to the city's housing problems Without this, it was argued, Sheffield would become too large, with the attendant problems of long and difficult journeys to work and difficulties of access for inner city dwellers to the countryside. A green belt ten miles deep was seen as appropriate for a city of Sheffield's size, beyond which a satellite could be contemplated. Finally the deputation urged that there should always be a suitable transition from town to country by the inclusion in peripheral building schemes of tree planting programmes and close control of building materials. Once in the Green Belt all buildings should be in stone with stone slates or the nearest equivalent.

The deputation was received 'in a friendly way' according to the Minutes of the Executive Committee in May 1957, and was told that the Town Planning Committee was in sympathy with the preservation of the Green Belt as a whole, but considered that there might have to be modifications. It was also made clear that there was no question of submitting a formal green belt scheme to the Minister, city-wide or jointly with the neighbouring authorities, until the Government circular had been discussed by a joint meeting of local authorities.

Throughout the rest of the 1950s the debate about extending Sheffield's boundaries and building in the Green Belt rumbled on, with a lively correspondence in the local press. At the same time the demand for land for housing was reduced by the City Architect's use of difficult and steep sites and by increasing housing densities. Even so, it was estimated that available building sites within the city boundary would be used up by 1962, with land for 24,000 houses still required. The threat to the Green Belt remained. This was exemplified by further threats of incursion at Middlewood in 1959 and at Redmires in 1960. In the case of Middlewood, where the Corporation wished to build 400 houses on 38 acres of Green Belt land, following a public inquiry in July 1959, the Minister rejected the application, but inferred he would consider an alternative scheme with fewer houses and more playing fields. The Redmires threat involved five acres of Green Belt owned by the Hallamshire Golf Club. The Corporation had decided not to object and at the public inquiry went to extraordinary lengths to support the private developer's case. The Minister allowed the development subject to certain conditions.

But it was not only Sheffield City Council that threatened to make incursions into the 'agricultural reservations' surrounding the city on the south, west and north-west as had been pointed out by the deputation to Sheffield City Council's Town Planning Committee in February 1957. In May 1956 it was reported that Chesterfield Rural District Council proposed to build a housing estate at Westwell Farm, west of Mosbrough, on what in Derbyshire County Council's Development Plan was designated as green belt land; and in October 1960 it was learned that Wortley Rural District Council was considering a compulsory purchase order for parts of Bitholmes Farm at Wharncliffe Side on the western side of the Upper Don Valley. In both cases the Branch resolved to oppose the developments if they were proceeded with.

More alarmingly, in January 1956 it was reported that because of the expansion of Samuel Fox's steelworks at Stocksbridge, there was a demand for 1,000 new houses, which would lead to further urbanisation of the Little Don Valley on the borders of the Peak District National Park. The Annual Report for 1956 described the appearance of recent housing in the Stocksbridge area, both private and public, as deplorable. By October 1957 it was reported that the West Riding County Council, contrary to its Development Plan, proposed to use 27 acres at Deepcar and 42 acres above Stocksbridge for housing development. The latter proposal meant that housing would be pushed into the Pennines near Bolsterstone, less than a mile from the boundary of the Peak District National Park. A public inquiry was held at Stocksbridge on 18 December, with objections from the Peak

Park Planning Board and the CPRE. At the inquiry, Gerald advocated the siting of any new development below the 850 foot contour, and thus out of view from the surrounding hills. The objections were in vain and letters written to both the County Council and Stocksbridge Urban District Council, once the decision was known, about design, materials and tree planting, received non-committal replies. Subsequently the Executive Committee supported the Don Valley Rural Amenities Association in its unsuccessful efforts to get the Peak District National Park boundaries extended to include Bolsterstone, Onesacre and Brightholmlee.

The Stocksbridge development was, in the view of the Branch, only the latest example of lack of architectural control in that part of the West Riding lying north-west of Sheffield. In the Annual Report for 1959 it was asserted that this countryside 'of bold uplands and woods' had been 'ravaged in various places by development as graceless as any that has yet appeared'. The report sited recent harm done to the villages of Thurgoland, Silkstone, Cawthorne, Higham and what was described as 'the murdered village of Stannington'.

Nor was it only residential development that threatened the remaining countryside between Sheffield and its neighbours. In 1955 an application was made to extend a rolling mill on farmland at Butterthwaite, Ecclesfield, in an area forming a narrow green belt between Sheffield's northern suburbs and those on the western side of Rotherham. The application was approved by the West Riding County Council, which admitted that it had not considered Butterthwaite to be an area of high amenity because of its proximity to industry. Wortley Rural District Council passed the application on the casting vote of the Chairman. Sheffield City Council objected to the proposal. Following a two-day public inquiry held at Grenoside in July 1956, at which Gerald presented evidence against the proposal, the application was turned down, the Minister (Duncan Sandys) stating that he had in mind 'the need to limit the outward sprawl of large industrial towns and to preserve belts of undeveloped land on their edge, even where this land is not itself of high landscape value…'. Six months later a new minister (Henry Brooke) allowed a new application from the same firm in an adjoining field across the railway line on the Sheffield side after refusing a further public inquiry.

The threat of new open-cast coal mining operations in the surrounding countryside continued throughout the 1950s. In 1953 vigorous opposition by Chesterfield Rural District Council and from the Branch helped to prevent open-cast coal mining operations in the beautiful Amber Valley near Ashover. In 1954 boring for coal took place in an area initially extending over 71 acres in the Rivelin Valley mostly within Sheffield's

Farmland in the Rivelin valley threatened by open-cast coal mining.

provisional Green Belt. This aroused immediate and unanimous opposition in Sheffield including the whole of the City Council and all seven Sheffield MPs. The Ministry of Fuel and Power resisted the widespread protest, authorised prospecting to proceed and good quality coal was found but further prospecting was required to ascertain if coal was present in sufficient quantities. The Branch and its allies continued to protest and in February 1957 it was announced that prospecting had been deferred indefinitely. In 1955 prospecting took place north of Dronfield Woodhouse in the neighbourhood of Mickley–Northern Common–Barnes Farm. It was the opinion of Derbyshire's County Planning Officer that amenity objections would not succeed and the Executive Committee decided not to raise objections but to press for the protection of amenities during the work and the drawing up of a restoration plan. A bitter blow came in May 1956 when it was reported to the Executive Committee in confidence that Mrs Bagshawe of the Oakes at Norton had been obliged, owing to heavy death duties, to allow Hazlehurst Farm and Delves Wood in the Moss Valley to be worked for open-cast coal, this being an area successfully saved in 1950, following a petition with more than 7,000 names. It was felt that in the circumstances it was not appropriate to object, but it was resolved, as in the case of the Dronfield Woodhouse proposal in the previous year, to press for the strictest possible screening and replanting conditions. Then in June 1958 authority was granted to prospect for coal in the Dyche Lane area north of Coal Aston and in the attractive Troway area further east, the latter area being referred to in the Minutes of the Executive Meeting of June 1958 as 'the most popular portion of the Green Belt between Sheffield and Chesterfield'. The Branch led the opposition, which was backed by local residents and Sheffield City Council and Derbyshire County Council, with press coverage in local and national newspapers. In March 1959 there was a Government statement that no fresh contracts would be let, no new compulsory purchase orders confirmed, and that the National Coal Board would not acquire land for such purposes when it would harm areas of natural beauty. But prospecting continued.

Another major threat to Sheffield's countryside, no less ominous in its potential repercussions than open-cast coal mining, was the proposal in 1959 by the Cleansing Committee of Sheffield City Council to tip crude refuse in an area of 50 acres in and around shallow quarry workings at Brown Edge. The site lay on the footpath to Burbage at the end of the footpath up the Porter Valley. Not only was the site in Sheffield's provisional Green Belt, it was in the Peak District National Park. The proposal was for tipping to continue for fourteen years with up to forty lorries a day entering the site. The Annual Report of 1959 said:

> *It is hard to believe that a Sheffield authority, guardian of the Green Belt, and conscious of what the peace and beauty of this place mean to its citizens could devise so unpopular a site for this purpose.*

The Peak Park Planning Board, which as is shown below, was repeatedly praised by the Executive Committee for its stand against countryside disturbance from whatever quarter in the 1950s, in this case, although it received the proposal with serious misgivings, suggested a compromise: five acres instead of fifty, screened by trees with a guarantee of no further encroachment. The Annual Report of the Branch for 1960 said this tactic was a mistake and went on to say that in the long experience of the Branch ' when the first aim is appeasement rather than principle it ultimately weakens our cause'. The City Council refused to accept the compromise put forward by the Peak Park Board. A public inquiry took place in Sheffield on 13 and 14 January 1960 with the Branch's case being put by Gerald. Five local amenity societies also objected to the proposal. The Minister duly refused permission for the tip, stating that on amenity grounds there was an overwhelming case against it.

Not only was the Executive Committee active in preventing incompatible developments in the countryside reservations around the city of Sheffield, it was also active in preserving traditional features. In 1957 Sheffield City Council's Parks Committee proposed to demolish Shepherd Wheel in the Porter Valley, a water-powered grinding hull for which records stretched back as far as 1566 and which had remained in operation until as late as 1930. After a prolonged campaign by the Council for the Conservation of Sheffield Antiquities, to which the Branch gave its support, the Parks Committee agreed that the workshop, wheel and dam would be spared provided the voluntary body raised the money for their restoration (about £500). The City Council agreed to be responsible for future maintenance of the site.

As it had done in the pre-war days in the Mayfield Valley, the Executive Committee continued to intervene to try to prevent the unnecessary demolition of old cottages, barns and farmsteads in the surrounding countryside. In 1957 Chesterfield Rural District Council condemned eleven cottages at Norton on the Bagshawe estate at the Oakes. A public inquiry was called and the Branch employed David Nye, an expert from the Society for the Preservation of Ancient Buildings (SPAB), whose opinion was that the cottages were basically sound and worth saving because of their appearance and historical interest. He stated that he was 'flabbergasted' that clearance orders had been issued 'in respect of properties in such good order standing in a park with plenty of space and light'. It also transpired at the inquiry that the cottages had been condemned without the advice of an architect. Mrs Bagshawe was also prepared to spend £500 on each to bring them up to the standards of the bye-laws. They were reprieved. In the same year the same threat arose at Holmesfield where eighteen cottages including a picturesque group opposite Cartledge Hall were threatened with demolition. Again a public inquiry was held with the Branch represented by the Chairman, Mansell Jenkinson. Permission for the cottages opposite Cartledge Hall to remain was given. Early in 1960 demolition notices were again served by Chesterfield Rural District Council on ten old stone dwellings in the Barlow district including the interesting Elizabethan houses at Barlow Grange. The Rural District Council refused to buy and repair the buildings but was prepared to give grants and extend the period before demolition. It was even suggested at this juncture that a scheme might be considered by the Executive Committee of buying one of the cottages, reconditioning it, and renting it to a rural worker, in the hope that it might serve as an example.

III

The designation of the Peak District as a national park in late 1950 and the creation of the Joint Planning Board did not mean that the Branch would or should pay less attention to issues in the Peak District. Nor was there any suggestion that the Voluntary Joint Committee for the Peak District National Park (which of course had been formed under the auspices of the Branch, and of which Ethel and Gerald were Joint Secretaries) should cease to exist. Indeed at the meeting of the Committee held on 8 September 1951 it was felt that it 'should not only continue in existence, but should increase its activities'.

Despite the Executive Committee's initial concern about the possible ineffectiveness of the Peak Park Joint Planning Board because of its membership structure, the Annual Reports of the Branch throughout the 1950s praise the Board's work. The 1951 Report stated that 'Much now depends on the personnel of the Board and the standards set at the outset'. Disappointment that only two members of the Joint Committee had been appointed to the Board was offset to some extent by the fact that Gerald had been made vice-chairman, an additional supporter, Professor A.R. Clapham, was appointed to the Board at its first meeting, and Mr A.L. Oldacre, for many years with the Peak Joint Planning Committee, had been appointed Planning Officer of the Park. The 1953 Annual Report praised the Board's effectiveness in protecting the limestone area of the Peak Park from industrial encroachment, its encouragement of good stone buildings, the removal of serious defacement, the preservation and planting of trees, the exercise of powers relating to access, and progress towards the setting up of a warden service. Throughout the rest of the 1950s and beginning of the 1960s, the Board continued to be praised for its admirable control of day to day building development. However, despite the early and continued confidence in the Joint Planning Board, the Branch's main centre of concern remained with the Peak District.

The possible extension of limestone quarrying remained the principal area of concern in the early 1950s. Between 28 October and 27 November 1952, eight applications for the extension of quarries were rejected by the Peak Park Joint Planning Board, and, although two were withdrawn, this left six public inquiries at which the Branch and the Voluntary Joint Committee would have to be represented. The cases in question were at

Gautries Hill, threatened by an application to quarry limestone.

Eldon Hill where Eldon Hill Quarries Ltd. sought permission to extend quarrying for another quarter of a century; Gautries Hill at the head of Perryfoot Dale where Derbyshire Stone Ltd wished to open up a new quarry; Sparrowpit Quarry where Derbyshire Mineral Mines had applied to extend their workings; the re-opening of a quarry at Cotterhole on the Via Gellia by the B.B. Mining Company; Hand Dale, Hartington, where Tarslag Ltd. sought permission to open a quarry; and at Parwich where Whitecliffe Quarries wished to resume working. After public inquiries in which Gerald and the geologist Edgar Morton presented evidence on behalf of the Branch and the Voluntary Joint Committee, the applications for Gautries Hill, Cotterhole in the Via Gellia, and Hand Dale were refused. However permission was granted for continued working at Eldon Hill and Sparrowpit for 44 and 43 years respectively, and at Parwich permission was given for large-scale working at a previously small quarry.

In the spring of 1953 the proposal to create a by-pass around Bakewell, a scheme which had first been proposed in 1936 but which had been abandoned in 1937, was revived by Derbyshire County Council with the support of the Ministry of Transport. The scheme was again opposed vigorously by the Branch and the Voluntary Joint Committee on the grounds that it would drive a wide road through the town's attractive river pastures, spoil the riverside walk to Haddon Hall, interfere with the show ground and destroy Scot's Garden, bequeathed to the people of Bakewell for their permanent enjoyment. It would also cut the access to the north of the town and to the railway station, involve the canalising of the River Wye, and shave the graceful approaches

Bakewell town bridge.

to the town bridge and the ancient packhorse bridge further north, destroying their symmetry and character. It was considered that the Buxton-Ashbourne road was a good alternative in summer, and in winter, when there was little traffic congestion in Bakewell, a by-pass was not necessary. No traffic census had been carried out in connection with the scheme. The National Parks Commission also objected vigorously, noting in their Fifth Annual Report that 'After an inspection we were in no doubt that such a by-pass would irreparably alter the character of the Wye valley at Bakewell and thus detract very seriously from the character and beauty of the town…' Bakewell Urban District Council also opposed the scheme as did many Bakewell residents.

For the first time since its inception, the Branch was in serious disagreement with the Peak Park Board over the scheme. By the casting vote of its Chairman (who was also Chairman of Derbyshire County Council and of its Bridges and Highways Committee), after a stormy discussion, the Board approved in February 1954 the inclusion of the by-pass in its proposed Development Plan. But before the scheme could be confirmed there would have to be a public inquiry. A three-day public inquiry eventually took place in early November 1956, with the Branch and the Voluntary Joint Committee represented by Mr Stanley Price, QC. Gerald presented evidence on behalf of the CPRE National Executive and the Standing Committee on National Parks, and Ethel presented evidence on behalf of the Branch and the Voluntary Joint Committee.

After four years, the Ministry of Housing and Local Government approved the inclusion of the by-pass in the Peak Park Development Plan, but the decision was not relayed formally to those objecting at the public inquiry, but leaked out in the press. Another (Ministry of Transport) inquiry was also scheduled, when a final decision would be reached. The scheme has never been implemented.

Another scheme that raised the unqualified disapproval and opposition of the Branch was the proposal by Derbyshire County Council to make a motor racing circuit in the Peak Park. The establishment of such a facility was approved in principle by Derbyshire County Council, as Highway Authority, on 4 May 1955. The proposed route comprised over four miles of the Buxton–Ashbourne road and the area eastwards towards Lathkill Dale. It was later amended to go westward into the upper slopes of the Dove valley above Hartington involving the opening up of the narrow lanes of Hand Dale and Long Dale. The Branch's opposition—for which it had the support of CPRE National Office, the National Parks Commission,

Long Dale, leading to Upper Dovedale, part of the proposed motor racing circuit.

the Nature Conservancy, the Ramblers' Association and a host of other national and local organisations—was based, naturally, on the presumption that the prime purpose of the National Parks Act was for 'the preservation and enhancement of natural beauty'. The Branch drew attention to the intrusion and disturbance such a facility would cause: structures such as pits, grandstands, lavatories and sewage disposal works; degradation of land by trampling; facilities for large-scale car parking (the figure of 25,000 vehicles was cited); obstruction to normal traffic; cutting off of farms during race meetings; disturbance by noise of the normal peaceful enjoyment of the countryside; and dangerous high speed use of the track throughout the year by irresponsible motorists testing the top speed of their vehicles. The fact that it became clear that preparations had been taking place in secret since 1953 was a further cause of hurt and anger.

The scheme became a national controversy. There was a debate in the House of Lords and questions were asked in the Commons. Newspapers such as the *Manchester Guardian* and the *News Chronicle* came out in opposition and there was even a leader in *The Times* opposing the scheme. *The Times* leader concluded: 'The preservation of open spaces as valuable as is the Peak District should not be tampered with to make a speed-merchant's holiday'. In the face of widespread and sustained criticism of the scheme, the steps to promote the Parliamentary Bill that would have been necessary for its implementation were not taken, and in January 1956 it was announced that the scheme had been postponed. Alderman White, the Chairman of the County Council, insisted that the project was 'dormant but not dead'. It has never been resurrected.

In July 1955 it was made public—at a Board meeting—that the Carnegie Trustees had made an offer to the Peak Park Planning Board of £35,000 for the erection of a tea pavilion and viewing platform at some beautiful spot at a high altitude which had previously only been approachable on foot. The new facility was to be approachable by cars and charabancs, and it was a condition of the offer that there should be unobstructed views on three sides. The original offer had been made late in 1954 but had been kept secret by the Chairman and planning officers. The rest of the Planning Board were presented with what amounted to a *fait accompli*, with a site selected near Eaglestone on Baslow Edge. Gerald strongly opposed the scheme at the meeting on the basis that it would destroy the essential wildness of a moorland spur at a height of 1,000 feet and visible for many miles around. He moved that the proposal should first be considered in principle. He was supported by the Ministerially appointed members but they were out-voted by the local authority members. The Branch sent the Carnegie Trustees a letter of protest (with photographs) but in the end the matter was settled without further argument or inquiry simply because the owners of the site selected by the Peak Park Planning Board, Bakewell Rural District Council, who had not been approached by the Board, decided by a large majority not to sell it. One Bakewell Rural District councillor said erecting a building on the site 'would be vandalism of the worst description'.

Another major victory in the mid-1950s followed a campaign to prevent the further opening up to vehicles of the foot track in the Manifold Valley that followed the route of the former light railway given to Staffordshire County Council in the 1930s. In 1952, against much public protest and with the acquiescence of the Peak Park Planning Board, the County Council had improved that part of the track between Butterton Station and Redhurst Halt (about 1½ miles), and made it suitable for cars. In 1957 the County Council proposed to open up a further 1½ miles to motor traffic in the most picturesque part of the valley—from Redhurst Halt to Weag's Bridge. The Branch's and the Voluntary Joint Committee's protests were joined by the National Parks Commission, CPRE National Office, the National Trust and the Ramblers' Association. In November 1957 the Peak Park Board opposed the proposed development and in 1959, in the face of continued widespread opposition, Staffordshire County Council withdrew its proposal.

No campaign was too small or too large for the attention of the Branch and its Executive Committee. At a small local scale the Executive gave its whole-hearted support to minor expenditure in connection with the work of 'voluntary assistance parties', usually led by Gerald, which periodically went out clearing up litter and repairing walls in the Peak Park.

At the national scale, the Branch supported the opposition to the construction of a nuclear power station at Trawsfynydd in the Snowdonia National Park and Gerald was Vice-Chairman and then Acting Chairman of the North Wales (Hydro-Electricity) Protection Committee in the critical period before the public inquiry in February 1958. The case was seen as a critical one not only for Snowdonia but for national parks in general and the Government's decision to sanction the scheme, against the advice of the inquiry inspector, was seen as disastrous.

IV

In any organisation that had been in existence for more than a quarter of a century, and in which there had been outstanding loyalty, it is hardly surprising that by the 1950s it was a regular occurrence for members of the Executive Committee to stand at the beginning of meetings to pay respect to Executive Committee members, ordinary members and supporters from other organisations who had died, usually in old age. The death of Mrs Ward has already been referred to above. But there were deaths of at least seven other people who had made outstanding contributions to the cause of countryside preservation in South Yorkshire and the Peak District.

From outside the Branch were Mr A.L. Oldacre, the Rev H.H. Symonds and Professor Sir Patrick Abercrombie. Mr Oldacre had been Planning Officer of the Joint Peak Planning Committee from 1935 and then briefly of the Peak District National Park. He died in 1953. The Minutes of the Executive Meeting of 29 September 1953 noted that 'his influence throughout had been strongly in accord with our views, particularly in regard to the improved appearance of housing in the Peak'. The Rev. Symonds, who died in 1959, had been leader of the Friends of the Lake District and a member of the Standing Committee on National Parks. He had been an ally of the Branch on more than one occasion and Gerald, who had worked with him closely in opposing the nuclear power de- velopment in Snowdonia, was present at the scattering of his ashes on Scafell. The sudden death of Sir Patrick Abercrombie in March 1957 was a great blow. He was chairman of the CPRE and its founding father. Called by some the greatest of planners, he had, of course, been responsible for the Sheffield and District Planning Scheme and was engaged as Sheffield City Council's planning consultant in 1936. In this capacity he had asked the Branch to draw up recommendations for Sheffield's Green Belt. He had also encouraged the Branch in the earliest stages of its work to promote a national park in the Peak District. The obituary in the 1957 Annual Report concluded that for those who had known him intimately, it was 'hard not to feel that the heart and soul of our movement has been taken away'.

Four long-standing members of the Executive Committee also died. Professor F.C. Lea, a member of the Executive since 1933, died in 1952; Mr W.A. Batley, who had been a member of the Executive since 1940 and who was a leading protester against open-cast coal mining at Wentworth, died suddenly as the result of an accident in 1953; and Mr W.H.S. Gibbs, a founder member who had played a vital part in the foundation of the Peak District Advisory Panel of Architects, died in 1958. The greatest loss was no doubt that of Mr G.H.B. Ward at the age of 81 in 1957. He was the 'father of the local ramblers' and a champion of the cause of natural beauty. The 1958 Annual Report carried a full-page picture of the man in his seventy-ninth year, preparing to search for a lost shepherd on Ronksley Moor. The obituary in the report pointed out that 'While our organisation was not yet in being, he encouraged the Hon. Secretary to found it; and from that day until his death he never hesitated in countless ways to further our cause.' He had left 'a blank that cannot be filled'.

G.H.B. Ward. (Sheffield Telegraph & Star)

The year 1959 saw the successful culmination of a long campaign to erect a permanent memorial to another well-loved local countryside lover, John Derry, editor of the *Sheffield Independent*, who had inspired many Sheffielders to know and love the surrounding moorlands. A public appeal had been made through the Branch before the outbreak of the Second World War to save the fine seventeenth century packhorse bridge spanning the Derwent near Derwent Hall, which was due to be submerged by the

Derwent Packhorse Bridge: above in its original location, and below during the opening ceremony after its re-building at Slippery Stones in 1959.

Ladybower Reservoir. In 1939, £1,000 was raised, the sum necessary to dismantle and re-erect the bridge elsewhere as the John Derry memorial. With the outbreak of war the scheme was mothballed, but not before the bridge had been dismantled, every stone numbered and safely stored. It was planned that after the end of the war, the bridge would be re-erected higher up the Derwent at Slippery Stones, where an ancient bridle track crossed the river on a concrete and iron bridge hardly in keeping with its surroundings. However, the scheme was delayed for a number of years because of the possibility of the further extension northwards of the Howden Dam, which would have meant that the proposed new site would also be flooded. By the time the reservoir extension was abandoned, the price for re-erection of the bridge had risen to £3,000. Generous grants were immediately forthcoming from the Graves Charitable Trust (£1,000); the Branch (£500); the Pilgrim Trust, the Derwent Valley Water Board, and Derbyshire County Council (£150 each); Sheffield YHA and North Midlands YHA (£50 each); and the Ramblers' Association (£25). A Branch member, Mr C. Brian Harley, also gave £50 in memory of his wife. The bridge was publicly opened on 26 September by Hugh Molson, the MP for the High Peak, who was also Minister of Works. On a glorious day several hundred people attended the opening, many of whom had walked south across the moors from Langsett and north from the direction of the Yorkshire Bridge.

7
Constant vigilance, expertise and onerous work
1961–1970

I

THIS DECADE WAS NOT ONE dominated by a few major campaigns but by a large number of cases covering, as usual, a bewildering variety of threats: proposed housing developments in green belt land, road widening, a proposed trans-Pennine motorway through the Peak Park, helicopter sites, tree felling, woodland clearance, open-cast mining, tipping, scrapyards, limestone quarry extensions, overhead power lines, reservoirs... The list is almost endless. The quotation providing the title of this chapter comes from the Annual Report for 1970 and neatly summarises the work of the Branch in the 1960s. Every possible violation of Sheffield's Green Belt and of the National Parks Act as it affected the Peak Park was watched in the most minute detail, the accumulated expertise of the Executive Committee was brought to bear on every issue, and for Gerald and Ethel, and a number of key members of the Executive Committee, this brought a heavy and unremitting workload.

As in the previous decade, the 1960s saw the loss by retirement or death, of key supporters. Professor Joseph Husband, the eminent civil engineer and member of the Executive from 1932, died in late 1961. He had given his expert advice in a number of important campaigns with an engineering aspect, for example a motor road through the Winnats, reservoir proposals in the Manifold valley, and overhead power lines, and it was his firm that was responsible for the re-erection of the Derwent Packhorse Bridge at Slippery Stones in 1959. In November 1962, the death occurred of Fred Marshall, MP, who had become a member of the Executive in 1936. He was a councillor, alderman and Lord Mayor of Sheffield, and as Chairman of the City Council's Town Planning Committee had played a crucial part in the establishment of the provisional Sheffield Green Belt in 1938. As MP for Brightside and Parliamentary Secretary of the Ministry of Town and Country Planning he continued to use his influence on the Branch's behalf. In August 1965 came the death at the age of 82 of J. Mansell Jenkinson, who had been Chairman of the Branch since 1948. An outstanding architect, Jenkinson was a great lover of the Peak District and its stone buildings and his own buildings carried on this tradition. The year 1962 saw the retirement from the Executive of Dr Edward Bramley, then 94 years of age, who had been a member of the Executive since 1934, and Treasurer from 1940 until 1947. On his retirement he became the first Vice-President of the Branch. He died in 1968 at the age of 100 and generously left a quarter of his residuary estate to the Branch.

J. Mansell Jenkinson, Chairman of the Branch, 1948–65.

Perhaps the most deeply regretted loss from the Executive in the 1960s, through a resignation rather than a death, was that of Alan Ward, Ethel's brother. He had gone to live at Baslow and found it increasingly difficult to attend evening meetings. He tendered his resignation in February 1967.

His contribution to the work of the Branch, particularly in the first two decades of its existence, was immense. Not only did he provide Ethel with practical support on surveys, he was Treasurer from 1932 until 1940, and provided substantial financial donations that allowed the purchase, usually for the National Trust, of stretches of countryside and individual farms in the Peak District.

There were also three other deaths in this period of individuals who had represented other organisations but who had also played an important role in the development of the Branch as one of the country's most outstanding conservation societies. In 1966 the death occurred of Phil Barnes who had been Assistant Secretary from 1930 to 1933 before leaving to be Secretary of the Lancashire branch of the CPRE. He was founder and leader of the scheme to organise voluntary wardens on the Longshaw estate for the National Trust. His brilliant photographs made an important contribution to the Branch's work in the 1930s and were still being used in publications and lectures long after he had left Sheffield. He had been awarded the MBE in 1961. An important supporter of the Voluntary Joint Committee for the Peak National Park, Mr H.V. Thompson, also died in 1966. A distinguished naturalist from north Staffordshire, he was Chairman of the Voluntary Joint Committee for nearly twenty years. In March 1969, the death occurred of Sir Herbert Griffin, secretary of the CPRE from its inception in 1926 until 1965. Ethel had worked closely with 'H.G.G.' in the immediate pre-war years when the concept of a national park in the Peak District began to take real shape. Some of the surviving correspondence suggests that relations were not always easy, Ethel not always being in sympathy with his somewhat neutral stance on some issues.

In July 1969 at a Special General Meeting in London it was decided to change the name of the CPRE. It was voted to change the name of the organisation to the Council for the Protection of Rural England instead of the Council for the Preservation of Rural England. The Executive Committee of the Sheffield and Peak District Branch did not agree with this slight change of name and made its view known to CPRE Headquarters.

II

There was hardly any point in time within the period 1961–70 when green belt issues were not before the Executive Committee. At the October 1961 Executive Meeting it was reported that the results of four public inquiries into proposed development in Sheffield and West Riding green belt land had been favourable to the CPRE cause. These ranged from proposed large-scale extensions to a farm at Bradfield, housing proposals at Parkers Lane, Dore and Myers Grove Lane, Stannington, and an application to extend a works beside the River Don at Oughtibridge. The Branch also objected successfully at this time to the proposal that a helicopter landing ground should be sited at Redmires.

While assiduously preparing evidence for public inquiries concerned with individual cases of incursion or expansion of urban land uses on green belt land, the Executive Committee continued to make the case robustly for a long-term strategic approach to Sheffield's expansion problems. In July 1961 the Branch President, Lord Chorley, the Secretaries, and two other members of the Executive Committee, Maurice Cole and Arthur Irons, went to London to put their views to the Local Government Boundary Commission. The main points made to the Assistant Secretary of the Commission were that it was the Branch's view that there should be no local government boundary changes; that a joint planning board should be formed to develop a common planning policy for the communities occupying the Don, Dearne and Rother valleys; and that the solution might be a new town or the enlargement of existing small towns outside the region. The case was presented more formally in a document drawn up by Gerald entitled 'The Case for the Planned Dispersal of Sheffield's Overspill to a New and Distant Centre', which was widely distributed.

In September 1962 the Local Government Boundary Commission's draft proposals were sent to the Branch for comments. Basically the Commission recommended that Sheffield should be allowed to expand in a south-easterly direction into north-east Derbyshire at Mosbrough and Eckington, and in a northerly direction into the West Riding at Stannington and Ecclesfield. The proposals disappointed the members of the Executive Committee in two important respects. First, the Executive Committee objected strongly to any further development in a northerly or westerly direction. This, it was argued, would inevitably take the built-up areas into what the Executive Committee called 'the precious and precariously reduced farm and woodland between the city and the Pennine moors'. Secondly, the Executive Committee deplored the fact that the suggestion that overspill from Sheffield should be accommodated in a distant new town instead of the 'piecemeal filling up of smaller rural areas' had apparently not been considered a better alternative. Gerald put the Branch's alternative views again at a conference called by the Local Government Boundaries Commission at Sheffield Town Hall in January 1963. The matter was not finally resolved until 1967 when approval was given to extend Sheffield's boundaries to incorporate 5,050 acres of land in north-east Derbyshire

Farmland below Birley Edge in the provisional Sheffield Green Belt.

including the villages of Beighton and Mosbrough. In January 1968 Messrs Clifford Culpin and Partners produced their interim report on the Mosborough (note the subtle change of spelling) Master Plan. Their concept, which we largely see on the ground today, was 'a cellular pattern of townships defined by a grid of primary roads at half-mile intervals'. The Executive Committee submitted detailed comments on the Mosborough Master Plan including a strong plea that the character of Ridgeway and the Moss Valley should be maintained, and that local building stone or Davie gritstone blocks (stone embedded in a concrete matrix) should be used.

In the intervening period housing proposals by private developers and by local authorities continued to occupy the Branch in its continuous campaign to maintain the green belts of Sheffield and the surrounding county authorities. The first case was the proposal by Sheffield City Council to build 3,300 houses north and west of Stannington including parts of the Rivelin Valley which had been asked for and rejected by the Minister of Housing and Local Government after the 1952 public inquiry. The Branch was accompanied in its objections by the West Riding County Council, Peak Park Planning Board, Wortley Rural District Council, Bradfield Parish Council, the Don Valley Rural Amenities Association, and the newly formed Stannington Association. A lengthy public inquiry was held between 14 and 22 April, 1964 at Stannington. The Branch was represented by Stanley Price, QC, and expert witnesses Gerald and Peter Macfarlane, the planning expert. The verdict, announced in January 1965, was largely in favour of the objectors. The Minister, Richard Crossman, said that the proposed building in the Rivelin Valley 'would involve encroachment on an area of very great natural beauty'

Spout House, Stannington, and its surrounding countryside in the West Riding Green Belt, lost to housing development by Sheffield City Council after the 1964 public inquiry.

and he was in no doubt that the Rivelin Valley 'should remain a permanent open space along the western approaches to the city'. He did, however, allow ten acres of encroachment onto farmland on the west of Long Lane, adjacent to the area in Stannington where house building was already taking place. He also allowed, to the huge disappointment of the Branch, the good farmland around Spout House to be taken out of the West Riding Green Belt, thereby, as the Annual Report for 1965 put it, ' thrusting an urban wedge into fine hill country verging towards the National Park.' However, Crossman stipulated that the layout, means of access, siting, design and outward appearance of buildings had to be approved by the Minister.

Between 1963 and 1967 the Branch fought a losing battle to prevent housing development at Wharncliffe Side on land that the Branch said was green belt and which Wortley Rural District Council said was not. The Minister of Housing and Local Government decided not to intervene and there was no public inquiry. The Branch supported Wortley Rural District Council at a public inquiry in 1964 concerning the proposal by the owner to develop Low Spring Wood at Bracken Hill for housing. The wood was an ancient wood in the West Riding Green Belt. The Minister refused the development.

Back in Sheffield in the autumn of 1964 there was what the Branch considered to be a serious departure from the City Council's Development Plan when thirteen acres at Burnt Stones, Sandygate, were abstracted from the provisional Sheffield Green Belt, without advertisement and without opportunity for public objection. The Minister refused a public inquiry and the Branch, through its Chairman, wrote a letter to *The Times* which was published on 27 October and which caused considerable interest in legal planning circles. The letter raised the question of the possible illegality of a departure from a development plan being allowed without a public inquiry, thus effectively stifling public objections before an impartial assessor.

Nor was it just proposed housing development in Sheffield's Green Belt that caused the Executive to spring into action. It was reported at the September 1964 Executive Committee Meeting that Sheffield Corporation proposed to use 104 acres of farmland at Redmires for controlled tipping. It was resolved to oppose this development on the grounds that it would permanently damage a beautiful part of Sheffield's Green Belt and the approaches to the Peak District National Park. A public inquiry was held at the Town Hall between 26 and 28 October 1965 where Gerald put the Branch's case. Other objectors included the Peak Park Board (one of whose witnesses was J.C. Wylie who had written part of the Branch's booklet on refuse disposal (see below)), the National Parks Commission and the

National Farmers' Union. The inquiry inspector in his report emphasised that being at high altitude and subject to strong winds, tipping at Redmires would result in paper blowing about on and beyond the site during tipping operations. The site would also be visible from the National Park. Reduced haulage times for refuse from the western parts of the city, he concluded, would not outweigh the amenity drawbacks. He recommended that permission should not be granted and the Minister refused planning permission.

In 1968 the focus returned to the West Riding Green Belt. In July 1968 a building company applied to build houses on 44 acres in the West Riding Green Belt at Thurgoland which might involve the construction of 400 dwellings, thus doubling the size of the village. Following a public inquiry in February 1969, at which Gerald represented the Branch, the appeal by the builder was rejected. In late 1968 the Statement for the Second Review of the West Riding County Development Plan was received by the Branch. The Executive Committee was very concerned that one of the proposed growth points was Penistone, which was intended to increase in population from 10,000 to 50,000. In the opinion of the Executive Committee this would have consequences which would adversely affect the Peak Park and it was planned to resist the proposal.

In late 1969 the focus returned to Sheffield with a jolt. It was reported in the Minutes of the Executive Committee Meeting in December that the City Council had approved for sale, for private housing development, 75 acres at Ryecroft Farm, Ecclesall, partly in the Green Belt and partly white land (restricted to rural uses), and a major departure from the City Council's Development Plan. A public inquiry took place between 17 and 19 November 1970 at the Town Hall. The Dore Village Society employed its own counsel and Samuel Furey, the Branch Chairman, and Gerald put the case for the Branch, independently of the Dore Village Society but in co-operation with it. There was some anxiety within the Branch because the Minister, Peter Walker, had recently upheld the appeals in green belt/white areas in three other areas, against the inquiry inspectors' firm recommendations. However, in March 1971 the Minister refused permission for housing development at Ryecroft Farm, agreeing with the inquiry inspector's conclusions that there was 'a very strong case against this development on environmental, amenity and hardship grounds, and in its favour only the argument of expediency'.

Ryecroft Farm saved from development following the public inquiry in 1970.

III

Despite the acknowledged continued excellent work of the Peak Park Planning Board—the Board was continuously praised in the Branch's annual reports for its 'admirable control' of development - ensuring 'a faithful pursuit of the purposes of national parks in the Peak District'— the Peak District National Park remained a central concern of the Branch. And as in the previous four decades it was quarrying and mining that came top of the list of issues with which it was concerned.

In 1961 the owners of Prospect Quarry in the Via Gellia, which was already regarded by the Branch as a 'disfigurement', applied to extend their operations by installing a very large screening and processing plant, in order to introduce a new system for crushing and grading. The application had been opposed by the Peak Park Planning Board and a public inquiry fixed for 30 November. The Executive Committee added its objections to those of the Peak Park Planning Board. Gerald represented the Branch and the Voluntary Joint Committee at the public inquiry. Mrs Pauline Dower, Vice-Chairman of the National Parks Commission, also spoke at the inquiry against the appeal. In August 1962 the Minister announced that he had rejected the appeal by the quarry owner.

In 1967 keen anxiety was aroused by a proposal to extend Lamb Quarry, a gritstone quarry on the roadside between Chinley Churn and the slopes of Kinder. The application was supported by the Peak Park Board on the grounds that further working of the quarry followed by landscaping would leave the site in a better condition than if it were abandoned in its existing condition. The Executive Committee took a different view and supported Chapel-en-le-Frith Rural District Council and a large group of local residents in opposing the application. The Branch's case at the public inquiry in August 1967 was presented by the Chairman, Samuel Furey, with the support of the landscape architect, R.B. Blayney. Unfortunately, the inquiry inspector agreed with the opinion of the Peak Park Board, and the Minister allowed the extension, although his generally unpopular verdict contained very strict conditions.

The Executive Committee was surprised to learn in late 1967 that T.W. Ward Ltd (the firm, it will be remembered, that was founded by Ethel's father) was likely to make an application to extend its quarry at Eldon Hill which had last been the subject of a public inquiry in 1952 where, in spite of widespread opposition, the firm had been granted permission to quarry for a further 44 years, on the strict understanding that the crest of the hill was to be retained. The new application, it was thought, would involve removing the summit. An application was made but was refused by the Peak Park Board, which made it clear to the firm that the present workings should cease at the appointed time.

Equally alarming as the proposed extension of quarrying at Eldon Hill, was the announcement in 1968 by Associated Portland Cement that it was intended to increase production at the Hope Valley Cement Works from 500,000 tons to 1,200,000 tons, making it the third largest cement works in the country. The increased production would be largely achieved, it was announced, by modernisation (two kilns instead of five) and the new Humboult process would practically eliminate steam and a new dust collection plant would reduce chimney emissions. The firm also emphasised that the extraction of limestone and shale would be kept within previously agreed boundaries. The firm also confirmed that there would be no change in numbers employed and that the railway would be used at a greater level for transporting cement.

The information provided by the company suggested that the modernisation of the plant and the increase in production would have little effect on the appearance of the landscape, but what bothered the members of the Executive Committee was that if production of cement was increased by 120 per cent, then limestone and clay would have to be extracted at a greater rate and inevitably the existing boundaries of the workings would

Eldon Hill Quarry in the 1960s.

be breached at some time in the future. They were concerned that more clay pits would then complete the ruin of the Hope Valley or be opened up even further afield, for example under Rushup Edge.

Along with 27 other organisations, the Branch objected to the firm's proposal and requested a public inquiry. Associated Portland Cement was strongly against a public inquiry because of the delay that this would bring to its proposed plans. As a result, with the help of local MPs, a meeting was arranged in June 1968 at the House of Commons between the Managing Director of Associated Portland Cement and Gerald, representing the amenity interests, a trade unions representative, Peter Jackson, MP, and Tom Swain, MP (in the chair). An agreement was reached at the meeting that the company would contain its shale workings within the 'Folly Ridge Line' to the north of the works and would give up its rights to work Marsh Farm and Brough Farm and any other areas in the Hope Valley outside the Folly Ridge Line. The company also accepted that it had an obligation to demolish the works and restore the landscape when cement production ceased in the Hope Valley. The company also agreed that distribution of cement by road would not exceed 570,500 tons in any one year and that a landscape scheme would be agreed between its landscape architect and the Peak Park Board. There were also other agreements about blasting and dust. On this basis, and provided the agreement was approved by the Minister of Housing and Local Government, it was agreed not to press for a public inquiry.

There were, however, two other public inquiries relating to mineral extraction towards the end of the decade. In September 1968 it was reported to the Executive Committee that Hoveringham Gravel Company had applied to extend its Outland Quarry in Smalldale and Littledale around Bradwell. There were already complaints of noise, dust, heavy traffic from lorries and large mounds of stockpile. The application to extend the quarry involved cutting through the skyline and exposing the workings from the high ground to the south. Three months later it became known that Thomas Marshall & Co had applied to extract fireclay on a prominent site at Delf Road, High Bradfield. The Peak Planning Board refused both applications. In both of the ensuing public inquiries, at which the Branch's case was put by Gerald (Outland Quarry) and Samuel Furey (Bradfield), the inquiry inspectors recommended that the appeals by the firms be allowed, but in each case the Minister dismissed the appeals.

Outland Quarry, Smalldale.

In November 1967 the Peak Park Board took the view that no further large-scale flooding of river valleys to create reservoirs should be authorised until all other sources of supply had been fully exploited. The Executive Committee was therefore 'stunned' to learn in the spring of 1968 that the Trent River Authority was planning two new reservoirs in the Derwent and Dove catchment areas and that seven possible sites were under consideration: Hassop, Turnditch, Ashover, Alport Dale, Black Ashop Moor, Winkhill in the Hamps valley and Brund in the Manifold. The 1968 Annual Report concluded that it was 'a totally unreal situation that a region should be secured…as England's first National Park and then that a separate authority should put forth proposals which would spoil its scenic value.'

Within a year Gerald had produced an illustrated booklet, *What Price WATER?*, which was launched in Buxton on 20 March 1969 at a meeting organised by Ivor Morten, Vice-Chairman of the Peak Park Board. Gerald gave an illustrated talk expanding on the ideas expounded in the booklet to an audience of 80 people. The booklet suggested reducing waste, using groundwater, abstracting and purifying water from the Trent and desalination of sea water as alternatives to reservoirs. After a lively discussion it was resolved that two messages should be sent to the Prime Minister and to the Ministers of Power, Agriculture, Housing and Local Government, and Technology:

> *THAT the losses incurred by the construction of further reservoirs in the Peak District, in homes, farmland, space for adventure, scenery and historic buildings and estates are too great to be entertained; and,*

> *THAT action should be taken at the highest level to set up alternative methods of supply and in particular a nuclear/ desalination plant to provide the water required by the Trent River Authority by 1977.*

Trent River Authority proposed the Hassop site for the Derwent reservoir and the Upper Manifold for the Dove. At Hassop, the owners of the land refused the request to make borings and following a meeting attended by 300 people at Warslow in November 1969, a Manifold Preservation Committee was formed.

Another continuous threat to Peakland scenery in the 1960s, and one that had been present from the foundation of the Branch in the mid-1920s, was disfigurement of the countryside by overhead electricity power lines. In February 1963 the Executive Committee discussed the proposed 400KV overhead power lines from Hunshelf to Stalybridge, which would inevitably involve great damage to Longdendale. The Peak Park Board had persuaded the Yorkshire Electricity Board to alter parts of the route, but the section from Dunford Bridge to Woodhead, the Board believed, should go underground. The Executive Committee supported this view. A public inquiry was held at Barnsley in October 1963 and Gerald not only represented the Branch's views, but also those of the Voluntary Joint Committee, and eight other amenity societies. He also walked the route with the two inquiry inspectors. The verdict was an outstanding victory for the amenity interests: for 3½ miles between Dunford Bridge and Woodhead, the electricity cables would be placed underground, in spite of very great expense.

In 1967 a similar case arose with the proposal to erect electricity power lines on 40 ft high poles from Scissett in West Yorkshire to Crow Edge west of Penistone. There was much local opposition with demands that they be placed underground, but the Yorkshire Electricity Board remained obstinate and the matter had still not been resolved at the end of 1970. Another proposed power line from New Mills to Buxton involved much delicate negotiation work from Gerald in 1968 and 1969. As a result, the Central Electricity Generating Board altered the route of the line in order

Site visit connected with the public inquiry into the proposed overhead power lines from Hunshelf to Stalybridge. The inspector is bowler hatted; Gerald is in the centre looking at the camera.

to reduce its effect on Whitehough village and agreed to plant trees to obscure the line from particular viewpoints.

Late in 1965 came the first suggestion that certain interests, for example, Sheffield Chamber of Commerce, were pressing for a trans-Pennine Manchester to Sheffield motorway which inevitably would cross the Peak Park (most probably over Woodhead), and in the opinion of the Executive Committee, have a detrimental effect on its scenery. There were lively discussions at the Peak Park Planning Board and at the Branch's Executive Meetings about such a road development and in June 1967 it was agreed that Gerald should draw up a pamphlet with illustrations against the idea of a motorway through the northern part of the Peak Park. Such a pamphlet did not make an appearance until 1974. Meanwhile the West Riding County Council was reported to be in favour of a motorway over Woodhead, whereas the Peak Park Planning Board had suggested a 'short circuit' connecting the M1 with the M62. At the Executive Committee Meeting held in April 1969, a resolution was passed, reiterating the Executive Committee's objection to a motorway through the Peak Park and asking the Government to wait to see what the impact the M62 had on trans-Pennine traffic between Sheffield and Manchester. It was further resolved that if the Woodhead route became inevitable, 'a substantial portion should be placed underground.' By June 1970 a White Paper 'Roads for the Future' had been published repeating the proposal for a strategic route over Woodhead. The Executive Committee repeated its objection and its suggestion to the Government. The debate had still far to run.

IV

Besides fighting particular campaigns, the Branch continued to pursue a policy of putting its principles and its aims generally before the public, as a way of not only recruiting new members and obtaining financial support for specific cases, but also as a means of influencing political opinion, locally and nationally. The term 'propaganda' was still being used in the annual reports in the 1960s.

In 1966 the Branch, through the work of Gerald, put together an exhibition of photographs showing the Peak landscape and architecture, together with examples of bad twentieth-century development. The exhibition was first shown during Nature Week at the end of April at the Pavilion Gardens, Buxton, with the event as a whole attracting 13,500 people. It was then on show in the Central Library in Sheffield throughout most of November with members of the Executive Committee acting as stewards and explaining issues to the public. It then went on display, in an expanded form, at the University library in January and February 1967. The three exhibitions were rewarded by a considerable increase in membership. Later in the year the exhibition went on display at Tawney House, Buxton, and in 1969 it was used to help in the formation of the CPRE East Riding Branch. In 1970 portions of it went on display at libraries in Derbyshire (Alfreton, Chesterfield, Clay Cross, Heanor, and Ripley).

The responsibility for giving lantern lectures had passed from Ethel to Gerald by the early 1960s and he usually gave between twenty and thirty a year to a wide variety of audiences, not just within the Peak District and South Yorkshire, but in various other parts of the country. The Annual Report for 1969, for example, recorded that in the last twelve months he had given talks outside the local area to Staffordshire W.E.A., Nottinghamshire Federation of Women's Institutes, Salford University, Wilmslow Townswomen's Guild and to CPRE branches in Lancashire, Oxfordshire and Shropshire.

In his capacity as President of the Ramblers' Association from 1963 to 1966, Gerald was kept busy preparing presidential addresses which gave him the opportunity to include references to subjects and issues of concern to both the Ramblers' Association and the CPRE. His growing national reputation also meant that he was invited to speak at a variety of conferences. In September 1966, for example, he addressed the British Association on 'Forestry in the Landscape' and in September 1969 he addressed the CPRE National Conference at Exeter on 'What Price Water?'

His most influential talk, however, was not given to a live audience but on radio. 'My case for preservation' was broadcast on the BBC Home Service on 20 January 1966 and repeated on 5 July 1966. It immediately brought telephone calls, letters and invitations to speak in various parts of the country. It was published in *The Listener* on 24 February 1966 and subsequently printed as an illustrated leaflet by CPRE National Office. Gerald's case was based on his view that human beings needed a direct personal relationship with their natural surroundings in which they could enjoy the grandeur of land and sea and feel the force of the elements. And yet in the twentieth century, he argued, people were surrounded in their daily working lives by ugliness and sameness, and there was a lack of balance in using resources. What was required, he went on, was a con-centration of industrial activity in prescribed areas and the preservation of the regional diversity of the English rural landscape. He realised, he said, that some would see him as someone 'swimming manfully against the tide of progress'. But he detected a movement in the tide of informed opinion in his direction. 'As a start', he concluded, 'let us restore the word "preservation" to an honourable place in our vocabulary.'

*'Man has need of a direct personal relationship with his natural surroundings' (*My case for preservation, *p. 3). Gerald practising what he preached.*

Two important illustrated booklets were also published in the 1960s. In 1962 *Progress in Refuse Disposal* was published, largely a reflection of the Branch's exasperation with local authorities' persistence in tipping rubbish 'in any convenient hole or depression', usually in the countryside and in Sheffield's case as recently as 1958, a proposal to tip within the boundary of the Peak District National Park. After a lengthy introduction by Gerald on present and alternative methods of refuse disposal, the second half of the leaflet consisted of a detailed description and appraisal of modern refuse composting methods by John C. Wylie, formerly County Engineer for Dumfries and author of two books on the subject. Then in 1969 Gerald produced his booklet *What price WATER?* through the Voluntary Joint Committee for the Peak District National Park. As already discussed above, the booklet was launched in Buxton in March 1969 in the context of the Trent Water Authority's proposal to build further reservoirs in and around the Peak Park. A year later Gerald produced an illustrated article on 'Reservoirs, for or against?' in *Country Life.*

V

The 1960s was Gerald's decade. He was at the height of his powers as Technical Secretary of the Branch (or Technical Adviser as he was called from 1965). He showed remarkable energy and performed on behalf of the Branch and the Voluntary Joint Committee in a variety of roles: expert witness, pamphleteer and public speaker being the most obvious. But it was his technical expertise in a very large portfolio of landscape and architectural matters and his highly developed organisational skills that made him the master of so many situations. And he had gained a national as well as a local and regional reputation. Besides his membership of the Peak Park Planning Board, he was President of the Ramblers' Association between 1963 and 1966, had become a member of the Yorkshire and Humberside Economic Planning Council in 1965, and Chairman of the Standing Committee on National Parks in 1968.

In this period he received two honours for his work. In 1963 he was awarded an honorary MA degree from the University of Sheffield. The public orator spoke of Gerald as the 'custodian of our natural beauty and arbiter of architectural elegance'. He went on to say that 'the energy and devotion which he has brought to his task have done much to make the Sheffield branch of the C.P.R.E. a model for the rest of the country.' Then in the 1970 New Year's Honours List he was awarded the CBE for his outstanding services to the Peak Park Planning Board.

Gerald receiving his honorary MA degree at the University of Sheffield in 1963.

8

A little self-congratulation
1971–1984

I

'ANNO DOMINI', IT WAS REPORTED in the 1982 Annual Report, 'threatens the stability of the office'. In fact the advanced ages of the senior officers of the Branch and some members of the Executive Committee, and among the general membership, had a marked effect on the Branch through the whole of the 1970s and early 1980s. Six long-serving members of the Executive Committee resigned: Ethel's sister and founder member, Gertrude, in 1975; Maurice Cole (member of the Executive Committee from 1931) in 1976; he died in 1980; Richard Endall (who had been an Executive Committee member since 1958) in 1980; Samuel Furey (who had been Chairman since 1966) in 1977; and Ted Spencer (who had been a member of the Executive Committee since 1947) in 1984.

But the greatest loss from the Executive through retirement was Ethel herself, who, as a consequence of advanced age (she was then 86) and indifferent health, resigned from the Secretaryship in July 1980. Ethel had been Secretary for 56 years. She then accepted the position of Founder and Patron. Gerald, himself aged 68, became Secretary.

The period also saw the retirement of Lord Chorley as Branch President in June 1975, after nearly thirty years in that post, followed by his death in February 1978. At a memorial service held at Stationers' Hall, London, Gerald, at Lord Chorley's special request, spoke of his devotion to the outdoor amenity cause (besides his Presidency of the Branch and his Secretaryship at CPRE Headquarters, he had been Vice-Chairman of the National Trust, President of the Commons and Footpaths Society and of the Holiday Fellowship). Lord Chorley was succeeded as President of the Branch by Sir Eric Mensforth.

The 'creative partnership': Ethel and Gerald.

There were also two changes of Branch Chairmanship in this period, and the long-serving Treasurer also gave up office. In 1977, Samuel Furey, who had been Chairman since 1966, and who had given unflagging service and whose legal skills had been put at the Branch's disposal at many public inquiries, was forced to resign through pressure of work. He was succeeded by Arthur Humphrey who was chairman until 1980 when he was succeeded by George Shaw. The following year, Arthur Irons, who had served as Treasurer since 1947, resigned from the post and he was succeeded by Derek Grayson.

This period was also marked by the deaths of a number of key supporters, in addition to those already mentioned. Dr L. du Garde Peach, the well-known author and creator of the famous Hucklow Players, died in January 1975. He had been a particularly good friend of the Branch over many years and had appeared in its support at a number of public inquiries. When the Branch was opposing the threatened motor racing circuit in the Dovedale area, he wrote and produced an uproarious comedy called *Speed the Plough*, which in the opinion of Gerald 'dealt a vigorous blow to this enormity'. In 1977 the death occurred of W.H. Wilcockson, the well-known geologist, a member of the Executive Committee for many years and of the Peak Park Planning Board. The Annual Report for 1978 announced the deaths of W.R.S. Stephenson and John Maidment, members of the Executive Committee for 30 and 20 years respectively, and of John Jenkinson, distinguished architect, son of the former chairman, Mansell Jenkinson, who had been a member of the Executive Committee since 1974. Another long-serving member of the Executive Committee, John Ardron, who had been a member since 1945, died in July 1978. This death was followed in 1983 by those of Sir Charles Husband, closely associated with the re-erection of the Derwent Packhorse Bridge, and Ivor Morten, member of the Executive Committee from 1960 to 1980.

The greatest loss was undoubtedly the death of Alan Ward, Ethel's brother, who died in March 1979. As has already been pointed out, he was a founder member of the Branch in 1924, had been a member of the Executive until 1967, and was Treasurer from 1932 to 1940. He had also been unstintingly generous in his financial contributions to the Branch. His contribution to the cultural life of Sheffield beyond the activities of the Branch was also outstanding. He had opened Ward's bookshop in Chapel Walk in 1929, and co-founded in 1936, with his brother-in-law, Sir John Rothenstein, the Sheffield Society for the Encouragement of Art, which he served as Secretary, Treasurer and President. He was also Secretary of the Sorby Natural History Society from 1932 to 1952 and its President from 1952 to 1956.

But it was not all depletion. New faces appeared on the Executive, some of whom—Shirley Foster, Roy Bullen and Jack Burling—would still be there at the end of the century. The death of long-standing supporters also brought unexpected legacies, the most generous being that in 1977 from Miss Gladys Wood of Grindleford, which amounted to more than £12,000.

In order to assist Ethel and Gerald with the heavy burden of the day to day running of Branch affairs, Jean Haywood was appointed in 1971 to join Jean Smart who completed ten years in the office in 1973. Jean Smart left in May 1975 and then returned in March 1976 after accepting one of the two new posts of Assistant Secretary. Jean Haywood, now the other Assistant Secretary, resigned in 1977, and from 1978 until 1982, when Lynn Hartley was appointed as Assistant Technical Officer, Jean Smart undertook the heavy secretarial work of the office alone, as well as assisting Gerald with public inquiry work and public lectures. The appointment of Lynn Hartley was possible through the launch in 1979 of a 'Survival

Alan Bassett Ward, founder member and generous benefactor.

Appeal' for £80,000 in order to provide a sufficient income to employ an architect/planner as a permanent technical officer 'firstly to assist and then replace Lt. Col. Gerald Haythornthwaite.' By the end of 1981 the appeal fund stood at over £41,000 of which £23,100 had been generously provided by Ethel and Gerald, the sum being part of the proceeds of the sale of Upper Booth Farm to the National Trust.

In 1974 the Branch celebrated its 50th birthday quietly and privately, when some thirty persons, members of the Executive with their wives and husbands, and the Branch President, Lord Chorley, gathered at the Peacock Hotel, Rowsley, for a dinner in honour of Ethel: not only had the Branch reached its half century but so had Ethel's tenure in the post of Honorary Secretary. Two years later the 50th birthday of the CPRE as a national organisation and of the Branch as the CPRE's representative in Sheffield and the Peak District was celebrated more openly. An exhibition was mounted in the Graves Art Gallery in Sheffield, and at the City Hall on 29 October 1976, an illustrated lecture, 'The Last Refuge', illustrating 52 years of campaigning to save the local countryside, was given by Gerald before an audience approaching 1,000. A collection was taken and raised £564. Fifty new members joined. Then in 1984 the Branch's Diamond Jubilee was celebrated, marked by the planting of 1,000 trees on the National Trust's Longshaw Estate.

II

Between the 1974 and 1976 celebrations, a major rift began to occur between the Branch and CPRE Headquarters. In February 1975, at the annual meeting of CPRE branches, the Director and Treasurer of the national organisation floated some ideas about the possible reorganisation of the CPRE and the substance of these ideas was reported on and discussed in CPRE bulletins issued by Headquarters in the spring and autumn of 1975. Basically, it was being proposed that there should be a centralised national registration of members by which means all subscriptions would be collected and handled centrally. Moreover, the existing system of representation on the National Executive would be changed: it would be elected from branch members by the branches at an annual weekend conference; representation of the constituent and founder bodies would end. The new Executive Committee would decide how the subscription income would be divided. Finally, branch bulletins, newsletters and annual reports would be issued centrally.

These proposed changes were not received favourably by the Executive Committee of the Sheffield & Peak District Branch. At the Executive Committee Meeting held in December 1975 it was resolved to send a letter to Lord Henley, the CPRE President, presenting, in no uncertain terms, the opposition of the Executive Committee to the proposed changes. The letter made it clear that in the view of the Executive Committee the changes would be so fundamental as to 'strike at the roots of the local interest in the protection of the countryside'. It went on to point out that when Sir Patrick Abercrombie established the CPRE he provided an Executive Committee with substantial representation from constituent bodies of national standing. This, in the Executive Committee's view, was the foundation stone of the CPRE's authority. But the position of the branches was different:

> *The branches were formed on a different basis and were primarily local societies subscribing to the objectives of the CPRE. They were federated to the CPRE but conducted their own affairs, built up their own funds and undertook their own campaigns. They drew authority from the CPRE and were geared through CPRE to the legislative and administrative functions of the Government.*
>
> *We consider this to be the most effective relationship between CPRE and CPRE branches and should continue.*
>
> *Local interest maintains our branch. The intimate relationship between our local membership and the branch office is an essential part of the branch's vitality. It is the local interest in the local countryside, and more often than not an affection for a particular part of it which maintains our membership and attracts new members and funds. The broad interest in the planning of the countryside as a whole is limited to a few cognoscenti.*

Centralisation of membership records or of membership circularisation, the letter went on, would destroy the contact between the Branch and its members, and if a central executive decided how subscription income should be divided, it would dry up the sources of money on which the Branch relied.

The letter concluded by reminding the national President that the Sheffield & Peak District Branch had been in existence under another name two years before CPRE was established:

*We have relied entirely on our own efforts for what we have
achieved for the last 52 years. Our accumulated funds have
been secured and accepted under the obligation to apply them
primarily to the protection of the area bounded by our set of
Rules which are of long standing. We could not therefore agree
to relinquishing our autonomy or the control of our members'
funds.*

The matter was discussed again at the Annual Meeting of branches in
February 1976, but there was little change in the proposals from London
or the views of the Sheffield & Peak District Branch. At the Branch's next
Executive Meeting in March a resolution was carried unanimously to
maintain all the objections made in the letter to Lord Henley in December
1975, and that if the proposals were implemented, to seek 'Association'
with CPRE but not seek representation on any re-organised national
Executive Committee.

In July 1976 a 'circular' was sent to all individual members and affiliated
societies appraising them of the proposed changes. The circular stated very
clearly that if the changes went through, the Executive Committee would
seek 'Association' for the Branch with the CPRE and possibly become
known as the Sheffield and Peak District Association of the CPRE. If this
were not acceptable to the national organisation, the Executive Committee
proposed that the Branch should secede from the CPRE and operate
independently under the title of the Sheffield and Peak District Society.
Members were invited to indicate on an attached proforma whether they
accepted or rejected the Executive Committee's proposed courses of action.
Members voted overwhelmingly in favour of the Branch retaining its
financial and operational independence. Just under half of the membership
responded (660 individual members and 28 affiliated societies); 652
individual members and 24 affiliated societies supported the Executive
Committee's views.

At the May 1977 Executive Meeting it was reported that legal advice
had been obtained about the Branch's position in relation to the proposed
restructuring of the CPRE. Legal opinion was that it would not be necessary
for the Branch to draw up an instrument of dissolution. It was a separately
constituted society with its own rules, which were a contract between the
Branch and each of its members. It was proposed and carried unanimously
that it should be formally recorded at the CPRE Annual General Meeting
later that month that the Executive Committee of the Sheffield & Peak
District Branch gave notice that it was not and could not be bound by the
terms of the revised CPRE constitution.

In August 1978 the Chairman of the CPRE, Roland Wade, wrote to the Branch underlining once more the view from Headquarters that branches should make a larger contribution to national costs. Headquarters had resolved that branches should establish targets and reach them by a variety of means—raising annual subscriptions and mounting fund-raising campaigns, for example. Arthur Humphrey's response as Branch Chairman, agreed at the meeting of the Executive Committee in October 1978, must have made gloomy reading for the national Chairman. It stressed that the members of the Executive Committee conceived it as their duty to devote the Branch's energies and money to protecting the local countryside. Any fund raising would be used to raise capital to employ another technical officer to assist and eventually replace Gerald. The Branch did not have the time to undertake special and continuous fund raising events for CPRE Headquarters. The letter ended by suggesting that Headquarters should consider reducing staff, reducing the range of their activities and moving out of London.

The matter rumbled on into the 1980s. There was lengthy discussion at Executive Meetings of the pros and cons of declaring independence of the CPRE. It basically came down to, on the one hand, losing the title 'CPRE' under whose banner the Branch had fought its campaigns since 1927 and, on the other, giving in to a mandatory increase in subscription or the transfer of accumulated funds to the national body. At the Executive Meeting held in October 1981 it was reported that the Financial and General Purposes Committee of the national body had recommended that branches should pay annually £2 per member into 'national funds' from 1982. This would mean that the Branch would have to pay about £2,000. In Gerald's opinion 'it was quite impossible' to accept that level of contribution to the national body. At the same meeting it was also reported that the Charities Commission, which the Branch had contacted for advice, had reported that in its opinion the Branch Constitution and Rules of 1931 (amended 1981) made the Branch independent of the national body under its revised constitution.

There was a frank exchange of views in the spring and summer of 1982 when in reply to a letter in January from the national Chairman, Roland Wade, the Branch Chairman on behalf of the Executive Committee, made it clear that the Branch did not feel it was bound by revisions to the national constitution made in 1967 and 1970 because these were made 'unilaterally'. In answer to the question asked by the national Chairman 'what is the Branch constitutionally?, the answer was clear:

> *...it seems to me that we are what we were in the first instance in 1927, and that is an independent body representing at their request the Council for the Protection (Preservation) of Rural*

England in Sheffield and the Peak District subject to Rules agreed by them in 1931, which ensure our operational and financial independence within the aims and objects of the national organisation.

The letter ended with the Chairman stating that in the Executive Committee's opinion the Branch should continue to operate under the title 'Council for the Protection of Rural England, Sheffield and Peak District Branch' as this was how it was registered with the Charities Commission and known generally.

Wade's reply in June was equally frank. While saying he regretted 'these exchanges' he pointed out a number of errors of fact in the Chairman's letter and drew attention to the fact that there was growing resentment on the part of a number of branches that some other branches were not supporting the national office as they should. He noted that it had been decided 'after all' to retain the word 'Branch' in the body's title.

The last exchange on the matter in this period was in December 1983, when in reply to a letter from the national Chairman in early December, the Branch Chairman wrote once again making clear the Branch's intentions: the Branch intended to remain an independent society federated or affiliated to the national organisation; it intended to control its own finances and to justify its support from local sources by work in defending the local countryside; and it intended to determine its own operational priorities.

III

Throughout the 1970s and the early 1980s, green belt matters consumed an enormous amount of time and energy of the small office team: monitoring planning applications, analysing and making representations and recommendations about planning proposals, giving evidence at public inquiries, and following up rumours and speculations, all undertaken with a meticulous eye to detail despite the volume of cases. In 1979 alone, for example, 13,000 planning applications were checked, the majority relating to the green belts around Sheffield and Rotherham. The main concerns remained as varied as in the previous five decades. These included the impact of road developments—in the late 1970s and early 1980s, the Stocksbridge by-pass scheme was monitored very closely; overhead power lines, with major schemes from Scissett to Crow Edge and Hunshelf to Neepsend (the latter running through Wharncliffe Wood) viewed with grave misgivings; caravan site proposals in unsuitable locations, with proposed new sites successfully opposed at Laughton en le Morthen and at Fulwood in Sheffield; and threats to woodlands, most notably woodlands in the Loxley Valley which were subsequently protected by Tree Preservation Orders, and Ecclesall Woods, where proposals to change the character of Sheffield's largest native broadleaved wood gave rise to the creation of a Woodland Advisory Group on which the Executive Committee was represented. The greatest concern, however, was the constant threat from housing proposals, large and small, on greenfield sites outside existing settlements, on the periphery of villages, and within villages where the danger was that village character would be diluted or obliterated.

With growing affluence, the extension of road networks (especially on the completion of the M1), and rapidly increasing car ownership, there was increasing pressure for residential development in the villages in South Yorkshire on the edge of and beyond the main urban areas, especially to the east of Sheffield and Rotherham. It was feared that such developments would be unrelated to the character of the landscape or to the local building tradition. The Branch intervened in 1972 over a proposal to build over 300 houses at Wickersley, and representations were made in the same year over proposed residential developments on land at Anston Hall, Firbeck and Aston. A public inquiry into the Aston application, which covered 37 acres of green belt land in a village described at an Executive Committee meeting as 'mauled and wrecked by new unsightly development', took place in December 1972 and the appeal by the developer was turned down. There were also fears for the character of villages to the north and northwest of Rotherham where they lay on or close to main roads and motorways. In late 1973 it became known that Rotherham Borough Council intended to amend its Development Plan to extend residential development north of the village of Thorpe Hesley. Gerald asked that the boundary of the development should be adjusted to fall short of Scholes Lane in order to preserve the rural character of the approaches to Wentworth Woodhouse and this was complied with. There were also fears for the loss of character in two other parts of the Wentworth estate at the end of the 1970s and in the early 1980s. Gerald was approached by villagers at Hooton Roberts early in 1979 about a development plan being drawn up by a firm of architects for Countess Fitzwilliam which was feared would result in large-scale developments in the village. He visited the village and subsequently wrote to Rotherham Borough Council pointing out that Hooton Roberts was in the middle of the Green Belt, and while the Branch welcomed sensitive renewal and use of existing buildings, it would resist any extension of the village. A 'highly satisfactory' response was received from the

The rural approach to Wentworth Woodhouse.

Borough Council stating that village renewal at Hooton Roberts would consist only of the rehabilitation of existing buildings contained within a tight boundary and precluding any development into the Green Belt. On the other hand, regret was expressed at the Executive Committee meeting held in July 1982 at the development of housing almost to the foot of Keppel's Column, at Kimberworth on the southern edge of the Wentworth estate, a familiar landmark visible from long distances. Rotherham Metropolitan Borough Council had refused permission for the development but the Secretary of State allowed it on appeal.

Nor was it just a case of residential development near motorways. In December 1970 the Branch had been among objectors at a public inquiry concerning an application to develop an industrial estate in the then West Riding Green Belt at Hellaby beside the M18. Rotherham Rural District Council was 'annoyed' by the Branch's opposition which was based on the fact that it was green belt land, that this 'out-of-town' development would affect the rehabilitation of surrounding towns and industrial villages, could be the forerunner of large-scale industrial developments at motorway interchanges in South Yorkshire, would lead to the deterioration of the landscape throughout the region, and might eventually result in the destruction of Hellaby Hall. The Secretary of State approved the application, his only condition being that there should be no substantial development around Hellaby Hall, which the development company involved had agreed to repair and use for a suitable purpose.

The Hellaby case underlined that the Branch continued in the 1970s and early 1980s, not only to protect the local countryside but also local buildings, and not just important country houses but also cottages built in local materials and in the vernacular style. In the first category, a particularly important case in this period was Thorpe Salvin Old Hall. In May 1977 the Executive Committee was informed that the Hallamshire Historic Buildings Society and Rotherham Archaeological Society had formed a joint committee with the aim of launching a public appeal to save the Old Hall, an impressive ruin of an Elizabethan manor house in private owner-ship, of which only the south facade and gatehouse had survived. The Department of the Environment had estimated that vital repairs would cost £10,000, and had offered £5,000 towards these, providing the balance could be raised locally. A member of the Executive Committee became a member of the joint committee and a leaflet about its aims was circulated in the Branch newsletter. In April 1980 the Executive Committee sanctioned the sending of a cheque for £150 to the appeal committee to complete the local £5,000 contribution to the repairs. At the other end of the conservation scale, a more modest set of buildings, Albion Row Cottages, ten stone cottages in the Rivelin Valley, were saved from a demolition order in 1974 through Branch intervention, and the five sitting tenants undertook recon-ditioning of the properties.

The Sheffield Green Belt and the West Riding Green Belt immediately north of Sheffield (large parts of which came within Sheffield Metropolitan District after local government re-organisation in 1974) were, like the areas to the east of the city, also both under constant threat from housing development throughout the 1970s and early 1980s. Among damaging developments successfully resisted included a five acre site at Brookhouse Hill, Fulwood in 1973; nineteen acres at Lower Hurst Farm at Birley Carr, eight acres in the Loxley Valley, and 25 acres at Windmill Hill, Chapeltown, all in 1975; another 25 acres in the Loxley Valley in 1976; seventeen acres in Worrall, and eight acres at Grenoside, both in 1977; fifteen acres at Wadsley in 1980; eight acres at Yew Lane, Ecclesfield in 1981; and eight acres at Chapeltown in 1982. North East Derbyshire's Green Belt also came under attack and successful campaigns resisted the development of an eight acre site at Eckington in 1976 and resulted in the deletion from the Derbyshire Structure Plan by the Secretary of State of a proposal for 1,200 houses in the Dale, Killamarsh, in 1980.

In 1976, Sheffield City Council arranged to sell 37 acres of land at Acorn Hill, Stannington, which it had acquired in 1965 for its own housing

The surviving Elizabethan facade of Thorpe Salvin Old Hall. (Joan Jones)

Albion Row, Rivelin Valley, Sheffield.

purposes, much against the wishes of the Branch, to a private building company. The original permission to build there, in what had originally been part of the West Riding Green Belt, had been given by the Secretary of State only on condition that local stone was used and that he approved the layout and house design. Having arranged the sale, the Council sought to modify the layout and design and use materials other than local stone. The Branch objected and following a public inquiry in June 1976, the Secretary of State turned down the modification order. In his report the inspector concluded that the implementation of a planning permission modified in the way proposed by the City Council '...would result in development very much inferior to that previously approved and of a standard unsuitable for this important site near the boundary of a National Park.'

The Branch's campaign against the use of inappropriate materials and colours, which had gone on almost since the first day of its existence, took an interesting turn in 1982 with the publication of an A4 four-page leaflet with five colour photographs entitled *The Misuse of Circular No. 7/77*. The issue which was the subject of the leaflet was the Government circular issued in February 1977 which appeared to give Crown departments exemption from the need to obtain planning permission. But as the leaflet pointed out, the circular also made it clear that Crown departments had agreed to inform local authorities where there could be visual impact from a Crown development, and it was then the responsibility of the local authority to decide whether to give the public the opportunity to comment and, if necessary, object.

What had given rise to the leaflet was the building 'in red-brick and even redder paint' of Middlewood Ambulance Station, in north Sheffield, by the Trent Regional Health Authority. The finger was pointed very publicly at Crown departments and local planning authorities. The Health Authority complained about the leaflet saying the Branch had overstated its case, and emphasised that the plans had been on public view. This was true, but the materials were said to be 'buff coloured bricks and dark brown paintwork'.

IV

It had been a bitter disappointment to the Executive Committee in the 1950s that Sheffield City Council had not established a permanent green belt as part of its Development Plan, as local authorities were invited to

do in the Government Circular 50/57. It was the provisional status of
Sheffield's Green Belt, which could be threatened not only by private
developers but also by the City Council, that had involved the Branch in
such a protracted campaign to protect it since its 'provisional' approval
by the City Council in 1938.

Sheffield's Green Belt remained provisional until the approval of the
South Yorkshire Structure Plan by the Secretary of State in late 1979,
which included broad provision for a green belt around Sheffield. Then in
October 1980, after pressure from the Branch, the City Council decided
to prepare a Green Belt Subject Plan. Gerald submitted representations
about the plan and discussed issues at the Town Hall with the City Council's
planning officers. The plan was approved by the City Council in December
1981 and submitted to the South Yorkshire County Council for certification
of conformity within the County Structure Plan. Overall, the Executive
Committee was of the opinion that the City Council had produced 'an
excellent document, worthy of praise and gratitude' but it objected to the
exclusion of four sites: Ryecroft Farm, Dore; Whirlow Hall Farm; the
grounds of Knowle Green House, Dore; and a large part of the Moss Valley
around Plumbley. The public inquiry was awaited with great anticipation,
although, as was the case with local plans, the inspector had no powers to
force a decision on the City Council: he could only make recommendations.

The public inquiry opened on 29 June 1982 and lasted until 23 July,
including five days spent visiting sites which were the subject of objections.
The officers of the Branch were heavily involved throughout the proceedings.
They and the rest of the Executive Committee and the Branch membership
as a whole were highly delighted with the inspector's report, published in
January 1983. He did not accept the House Builders' Federation's claim
that the Green Belt had been drawn so tight that it did not give adequate
room for residential development. In the eleven instances where developers
or landowners had objected to sites being included in the Green Belt, the
inspector remained firm, and turned down every objection. And three of
the four sites that the Branch had recommended should be added to the
Green Belt—Ryecroft Farm, Whirlow Hall Farm and the area around
Plumbley in the Moss Valley—were recommended for inclusion by the
inspector. He summarised his argument as follows:

> *The green belt is already tightly drawn and the effect of my
> recommendations is to make it somewhat tighter...*
>
> *Foremost among the reasons for having the green belt tightly
> drawn is the remarkable quality of the landscape on all sides
> of the city but the east. It is a landscape of bold relief with*

spurs of high land separating valleys which are often deep and which provide natural 'green wedges' into the built-up area. The countryside adjoining fulfils magnificently the function of a green belt to provide open country and outdoor recreation within easy reach of people's homes...Although I was concerned to secure if possible the exclusion from the green belt of some small areas of land on the west side of the city in order to provide for the possibility of a wider choice of housing, I was unable to do this; all the relevant objection sites belong naturally to unspoilt areas rather than to areas which are already substantially built up.

The inspector also recorded at the beginning of his report that the principle of a green belt almost encircling the city was long established. The 1983 Annual Report noted: 'We may allow ourselves a little self-congratulation in that this is due to a large extent to the work of this Branch.'

In May 1983 the City Council published its response to the inspector's report: it accepted all 34 of the inspector's recommendations except for three which it accepted only in part. One of these related to Ryecroft Farm,

Inspector's visit to Ryecroft Farm, Dore, during the Sheffield Green Belt public inquiry, 1982. Lynne Crowe (then Hartley) is at the back of the group and to her left is Jean Smart.

Dore, where the City Council had given planning permission for residential development on eight acres on the corner of the site shortly before the public inquiry began. Despite further protestations from the Branch, the City Council refused to change its mind about this modification. The Green Belt Plan, only very slightly modified from the inspector's recommendations, was adopted by the City Council as a statutory local plan on 30 November 1983 and it became operative from 5 December 1983.

At last, permanent protection had been given to the countryside surrounding Sheffield until the Green Belt Review of 1996. On the eve of the Branch's Diamond Jubilee year, 45 years of campaigning by the Branch had finally paid off. To celebrate the culmination of its long campaign, Gerald, with the assistance of Lynn Crowe (as Lynn Hartley had now become) and Jean Smart, wrote *The Story of Sheffield's Green Belt and a Guide to its Future*, a 48-page colour-illustrated booklet, which was published in 1984.

V

The Peak Park Board, from which Gerald finally retired in 1977 after 25 years, during which time he was Vice-Chairman for four years, Vice-Chairman of the Development Control Committee for nineteen years, and Chairman of the Planning Committee for two years, continued to be praised in the Annual Reports of the Branch for its 'competence', 'devotion' and 'ceaseless vigilance' without which, it was admitted, the Branch's efforts would have far less hope of success. On every possible occasion, especially during the period preceding the framing of the Local Government Bill (1972), the Branch, through its publications and through personal contact of its officers with MPs, ministers and government officials, emphasised that the great respect in which the Board was held was the result of its independence from county and county borough authorities. In the Annual Report for 1977 it was even suggested that Planning Board members and staff should have a special decoration 'for gallantry under heavy and prolonged political abuse'!

The Branch, usually in close support of the Peak Park Board, continued to keep a close eye throughout the 1970s and early 1980s on planning applications covering the same wide range of threats to the landscape as in the previous five decades. According to the 1973 Annual Report the 'prime danger' to the Peak Park was the urge for people working in the surrounding towns and cities to use it as a dormitory. The exorbitant price of land tempted owners to sell and the danger was 'obvious and imminent'. Nowhere was the danger greatest than in the Hope Valley, where, the Report went on, without stringent control, there would be one continuous suburb from Hathersage to Castleton. The renewed warning was being made because of the application by a local building firm in November 1972 to develop six acres near the Rising Sun Hotel between Bamford and Hope. The application was refused and then withdrawn. Other applications for outline planning permission for residential development were vigorously opposed, for example one for 69 houses in Eyam which would have completely altered the rural character of the village.

The Trent River Authority's search for at least one new reservoir site, begun in the 1960s, continued in the 1970s. An inquiry into the exploration of sites at Hassop and Carsington was held in September 1971 in Buxton. Gerald argued that the Hassop site was 'so patently contrary to the public interest that the exploration was a waste of money'. The application to make investigations at the Hassop site, to the great relief of the members of the Executive Committee and the Voluntary Joint Committee for the Peak National Park, was rejected, but permission was given to bore at the Carsington site. Because of the beauty of the Carsington site and its proximity to the National Park, the Voluntary Joint Committee decided to continue to oppose its use for a reservoir.

The Branch not only praised the work of the Peak Park Board in its development control work but also in recreation and education. In 1972, for example, the Annual Report praised the development of the 'delightful' Tissington Trail on the route of the old light railway from Buxton to Ashbourne, and the conversion of Losehill Hall into a field study centre. In 1977 the Annual Report applauded the Board's 'excellent' traffic management schemes in the Goyt Valley and in the Winnats. But they did not applaud every recreational initiative. The 1977 Annual Report was critical of the erection of information/interpretive centres in Dovedale and at the Magpie Mine, Sheldon. They were reckoned to be misconceived. It was argued that they would not only damage memorable landscapes but would increase concentrations of visitors and their cars in sensitive areas of the countryside. The same Report considered that the granting of licences for hang gliding on Stanage Edge to be 'imprudent' on the grounds that they would lead to 'great disturbance in this naturally majestic part of the Park'. The members of the Executive Committee also found 'worrying' some aspects of the Upper Derwent Management Scheme, when it first came to their notice in July 1978, and it was agreed that the Board should be asked if they could be consulted. The provision of a cycle hire centre at Fairholmes, which it was believed would cause great congestion, was

Proposed reservoir site, Hassop.

of particular concern. In January 1980, Gerald reported to members of the Executive Committee that on their behalf he had formally objected to the scheme 'as an undue regimentation' of the public's enjoyment of the area and to the detriment of quiet recreational use of the valley. Specific objections were made to the prevention of the use of green verges for casual parking and picnicking, the provision of a central car park at Fairholmes, traffic restriction orders between Fairholmes and King's Tree on Sundays and Bank Holidays, the establishment of a cycle hire centre there, and what was considered to be the unnecessary way-marking of routes for walkers and horse riders. The objections were unsuccessful.

The impact of limestone quarrying and mineral workings in general on the landscape of the Peak District continued to be a major preoccupation of the Branch in this period. In the 1970s particular concern was expressed over the impact of the extraction of fluorspar within the national park.

Laporte fluorspar workings on Longstone Edge.

Fluorspar, most readily obtained from old lead workings and spoil heaps, was in considerable demand as a flux in steel-making, in non-ferrous metallurgy and in the ceramic and chemical industries. Its production had greatly increased since 1964 when Laporte Industries started its plant above Stoney Middleton. In 1972 there were two applications to extract fluorspar west of the Heights of Abraham near Bonsall and extensive exploration for fluorspar was known to be taking place elsewhere. The disposal of the waste products from fluorspar extraction (tailings) threatened, in the view of the Executive Committee, to disfigure Derbyshire's limestone uplands 'extensively, rapidly and permanently'. Laporte Industries, which already had three tailings lagoons, was anxious to construct another, which would cover 70 acres, in Blakedon Hollow above Coombs Dale and a public inquiry took place in the autumn of 1975. Gerald and Stephen Morton represented the Branch and the Voluntary Joint Committee, and argued that a different if more expensive waste disposal method should be used—filter pressing, which resulted in a dry, stable, waste product that could then be returned to disused quarries and other mineral excavations. The Secretary of State, although stating that alternative methods of waste disposal must be found in the future, approved Laporte's application. He said the site was not of critical importance because it was not visited by motor borne visitors. It was not until 1978 that the Executive Committee felt that any notable advance had been made in the control of fluorspar workings. In September of that year, the Peak Park Planning Board approved the application of Dresser Minerals Inc. to excavate fluorspar off Conksbury Lane, Youlgreave, subject to the conditions that there should be a financial guarantee to ensure rapid and complete restoration of the site, and an obligation to use dry materials to fill the excavations thus involving the installation of a de-watering plant.

The scale of limestone quarrying in the Peak District in the 1970s and early 1980s also continued to cause great anxiety to the Executive Committee in spite of the persistent efforts of the Peak Park Planning Board. The Peak Park Planning Board's Development Plan (First Review) published in 1966, calculated that the annual production of limestone inside the Park had doubled from about one and a half million tons in 1955 to over four million tons in 1966. By the early 1970s the Branch reckoned that production was about five million tons. What this meant, according to the 1973 Annual Report, was that a piece of the Peak Park two miles long by 100 feet high and 66 feet wide was being removed on an annual basis. The Branch called for an independent committee to examine the siting of workings, methods of extraction, disposal of waste, storage of saleable stone, emission of dust and smoke, heavy lorry traffic, and the restoration and landscaping of workings and spoil heaps.

The results of campaigns to counter the limestone quarrying threat were mixed. In March 1972, following a public inquiry in June and July 1971, at which Samuel Furey and John Maidment had presented objections on behalf of the Branch, the Secretary of State dismissed the appeal of Hoveringham Stone Company against two Enforcement Orders by the Peak Park Planning Board. The effect was to oblige the firm to stop using an exposed site on Outlands Road, Bradwell, for storing saleable stone (40,000 tons of stone had to be removed), and to cease using the head of Hartle Dale for the tipping of limestone waste and to restore the tipping site. Then in 1973 it became known that ICI proposed to extend their Tunstead Quarry, near Buxton, eastwards into the Peak Park. This quarry was already said to be the largest in Europe, and the proposed extension would almost double it in size, and in the words of the 1974 Annual Report, destroy 'the peace and pleasantness of the beautiful village of Wormhill'. In November 1973 a deputation from the Branch was invited to the Buxton offices of ICI and shown in detail the plans for the extension and measures to screen the workings by tree planting. This did not change the Branch's opinion and official objections to the plan were lodged. A public inquiry, lasting well over a month, eventually took place in 1976. There was then a delay of about two years before the Secretary of State made his decision— the hope being that the delay meant that the Department of the Environment was giving serious thought to the use of materials other than limestone for roadstone and aggregates. However, on 8 May 1978, the Secretary of State approved the quarry extension, a disheartening decision for the Branch. At the very end of the period considered here, two major applications were being objected to: Tarmac Roadstone Ltd had applied to extend its Topley Pike Quarry near King Sterndale and T.W. Ward Roadstone had applied to extend the area of Eldon Hill Quarry and to continue quarrying beyond the time limit of 1996, which had been set by a Minister's decision in 1953.

VI

For most of the 1970s there remained the threat of a trans-Pennine motorway routed through the northern part of the Peak District National Park, and the possibility continued to generate the stoutest of objections from the Executive Committee, re-emphasising the objections made throughout the second half of the 1960s. The Annual Report for 1972, for example, made general objections to motorways in national parks, which, it was stated, would be 'a sure way to tame and abstract the romance from wild scenery' and would 'thwart the very purpose of National Parks'. Then, more specifically, the Executive Committee's proposal that nothing should be decided until an evaluation was made of the impact of the opening of the M62, was restated, given extra strength with evidence about the influence of the M62, following the opening at the beginning of August 1971 of the 28-mile stretch from Outlane near Huddersfield to Eccles west of Manchester. The point was made that since the opening of this stretch of the M62, the accident rate on the A628, the projected route of the Manchester to Sheffield motorway, had seen a 'remarkable drop'. This had been caused partly, it was believed, by the mild winter of 1971/1972, but also probably because heavy vehicles were leaving the A628 for the M62. It was predicted that a further reduction of traffic on the A628 would take place when the remaining length of the M62, from Outlane to Gildersome, was completed by the end of 1972. To drive home the general and specific points, the inside of the cover of the report contained two photographs of the M62 with the caption 'A foretaste of the devastating effect that a motorway would have on Woodhead Pass, in the Peak District National Park'.

At the Branch's Annual General Meeting in June 1973, held at Hope Valley College, the guest speaker was J. Lewis Womersley, the eminent transport planner. His title was 'Road Traffic in National Parks'. He covered a number of themes including the kind of road access appropriate to national parks, the lack of policies and principles in road design, lack of consultation and co-ordination between those responsible for national parks and highway planning, the concept of a road hierarchy with modification of highway engineering standards according to environmental settings, segregating different types of traffic, and the role of public transport. On the subject of the proposed Manchester to Sheffield motorway, he said the motto when faced by such an environmental threat, must be 'When in the slightest doubt, don't build'. He concluded by saying

> *There are two qualities which seem to be sadly lacking in many of those in positions of authority today—the first is common sense and the second is imagination. It is up to bodies such as yours to see that these qualities are injected. In concluding, therefore, I take this opportunity of paying a warm tribute to two persons who are spending much of their lives doing just that—and with very considerable success—Gerald and Ethel Haythornthwaite.*

The whole address must have been music to the ears of Gerald, Ethel and members of the Executive Committee. By October the talk had been published by the Branch as a small booklet (1,000 copies) and was widely distributed.

On 6 March 1974 a public meeting was organised by the Executive Committee in Sheffield to discuss the proposed motorway. It was attended by about 350 people including a coachload from Manchester. It was chaired by Lord Molson, President of the CPRE, who had for a long time been a keen supporter of the Branch and the Voluntary Joint Committee. At this meeting Gerald explained the background to the proposed motorway scheme and the Branch's objections to it. It was at this meeting that his illustrated booklet *A Motorway in a National Park*, published by the Voluntary Joint Committee for the Peak National Park, was launched. The main thrust of the booklet was the alien nature of a motorway in a national park: 'The din, stink and feverish movement of the motorway traffic would drive out peace'. Accompanied by striking photographs, including the famous one where a motorway was superimposed on the Etherow Gorge, Gerald examined in detail the impact of such a routeway would have on the landscape, the strength of the case in its favour, and alternative trans-Pennine routes between Sheffield and Manchester with particular emphasis on the railways. The booklet ended with the author addressing a number of uncomfortable questions. Wasn't Longdendale already ruined by reservoirs, road and railway and overhead powerlines? Wouldn't the motorway provide good

The basin of the River Etherow (top) with Gerald's famous superimposition of the M62 Rakewood Viaduct (bottom).

views and increase public enjoyment? Aren't the bridges and viaducts on motorways works of contemporary art and an inspiration in themselves? True in fact in all three cases, admitted Gerald, but false in conclusion. In Longdendale the road, railway and reservoirs were accommodated in the topography and the power lines were erected after the designation of the park and against the wishes of the Peak Park Planning Board; landscape could not be appreciated when travelling at motorway speeds; and the viaducts and bridges were not visible from the motorway and failed as works of architecture because they were not related to their surroundings. He was able to list more than 30 organisations who were objecting to the proposed scheme.

The evening ended with the Branch Chairman, Samuel Furey, proposing a resolution that the meeting should register its objection to the proposed motorway and inform the Secretary of State for Environment of that objection. It was seconded by Dr Frank Head, Chairman of the Voluntary Joint Committee, and carried 'enthusiastically', only three votes being registered against it.

The Government then announced that a consultative document would be issued in the summer of 1975 setting out alternative routes for the motorway and that public views would be invited. The Executive Committee felt that issues had been pre-judged by the recent promotion of a Denton relief road and a Hyde by-pass. These, they argued, were the first leg of the Manchester to Sheffield motorway. At a public inquiry held in the summer of 1975, at which Gerald represented the Branch and the Voluntary Joint Committee, it was agreed by the Road Construction Unit that the Denton relief road would be too big if the Manchester to Sheffield motorway were not built. It was also pointed out at the inquiry that traffic between Manchester and Sheffield was 'nowhere near' motorway capacity.

Victory for the opponents of the proposed motorway came in 1977 when the Minister of Transport, William Rodgers, decided not to proceed any further with the proposal. In his announcement, which was a surprise to the objectors, the Minister said:

> *On economic grounds, the building of a new road cannot be justified...I hope this decision will also be welcome to those who were unhappy on environmental grounds about the building of a new road through the Peak District National Park.*

VII

From its inception the Branch had been concerned not just with preserving the existing landscape but also with the quality of new buildings in the landscape and with the restoration of the landscape and buildings in the landscape. In the pre-war period the Branch's concern with buildings in the landscape saw the setting up of the Advisory Panel of Architects and the publication of a number of important practical manuals on design, layout and choice of materials. The year 1982 saw another important innovation in this general area of concern: the first Merit Awards for creative work which contributed to the quality and appearance of the landscape (including townscapes) or maintained the inherent beauty of the landscape within the Branch's area. The awards were presented by the Duchess of Devonshire at the 1983 Annual General Meeting. In that first year, there were five award winners in the architectural section: Thorpe and Associates, architects responsible for the restoration of the seventeenth century Oaks Farmhouse at Midhopestones; Glossop, Brayshaw and Bailey, architects responsible for the renovation and restoration of St Michael's School, Hathersage; Derbyshire County Council's Architects' Department for the new extension to Eyam School; the National Trust for the complete re-building of the barn at Heybridge Farm, Bamford; and the Peak Park Planning Board for the re-building of the Gatehouse at South Church Street, Bakewell. There was just one award in the landscape section: the Peak Park Planning Board for the landscape and improvement work at North Lees camp site, Hathersage.

Letwell Dovecote, restored by Letwell Parish Council, Merit Award winner, 1983.

9
The end of an era
1985–1995

THIS WAS A TURBULENT DECADE in which the intense activity of the past was continued unabated, when the geographical area of responsibility was widely expanded, and during the latter half of which there was a rapid turnover of technical staff. There was also a change of President and Chairman, and the resignations and deaths of some key supporters. But the two events that reverberated most strongly throughout the Branch office and the Executive Committee, throughout the membership at large, and into the surrounding region and beyond, were the deaths of Ethel and Gerald, one near the beginning of the period, the other marking its end.

Ethel died on 11 April 1986, aged 92, after a long period of indifferent health. She had resigned as Secretary as recently as 1980, after 56 years. The term 'Hon. Secretary', hardly does her contribution justice. It was immense. Without formal training, within a context at the outset in which countryside campaigning and conservation were the exception rather than the rule (the CPRE, of course, did not yet exist, and the only National Trust property in the Peak District was Winster Market Hall), when regional, rural and urban planning as we know them today were in their infancy, she appeared, aged thirty, fully equipped for the immense job before her. The principles which underpinned her approach were in place and unshakable, right from the start; her tactical skills and strategic thinking were razor sharp; she had no problem in embracing the long view; she was persuasive and was an excellent 'propagandist'; she had influence; and through her family background, and with the unselfish assistance of her mother, brother Alan and sister Gertrude, she had the financial resources to launch and sustain a life-long campaign. And she lived to see a successful conclusion to her two major campaigns, the creation of a National Park in the Peak District and the designation of a permanent Sheffield Green Belt.

Ethel, at the height of her powers, addressing the Ramblers' Association rally in Cavedale in 1951.

Gertrude Ward (left) with Ethel at Endcliffe Vale House.

And of course, in 1935, she had made an inspirational appointment to her staff, in the young and inexperienced Gerald Haythornthwaite. It must not be forgotten that she was his mentor and guide in the early years. She was a unique figure.

Only three years after Ethel's death, came the death of her sister Gertrude at the age of 94. Gertrude was a founder member of the Branch and served on the Executive Committee from 1927 to 1975. She was unstintingly generous during her lifetime in supporting Branch campaigns and supervising the domestic arrangements at Endcliffe Vale House until 1956, so freeing Ethel from domestic worries. She left £172,000 to the Branch in her will.

Other key figures also died in this period. Stephen Morton died in 1988. He had been a member of the Branch since 1936 and a member of the Executive Committee since 1946. Richard Endall, another long-time member of the Branch and Executive Committee member for 22 years before retiring in 1980, died in September 1989. His death was closely followed by that of Arthur Irons in December 1989. Arthur had been a member of the Branch since 1935, a member of the Executive Committee for 48 years and Honorary Treasurer from 1947 to 1981. The Annual Report for 1991 recorded the death of Professor Roy Clapham, renowned biologist, member of the Branch for 40 years, and who was for several years Chairman of the National Trust's Longshaw Estate Management Committee. The same Report also recorded the death of Dr Leonard Taitz who had served on the Executive Committee for fourteen years. Finally, the Annual Report for 1992 recorded the death of Lord Molson of the High Peak. He had served as MP for the High Peak from 1939 to 1960 and was created a life peer in 1961. He was a long-time member of the Branch, and had given his time and name in support of a substantial number of campaigns.

Annual reports also recorded the deaths of ordinary members, many of whom were extremely generous in the gifts they left in their wills. In addition to the magnificent legacy of £172,000 bequeathed by Gertrude Ward, there were many others ranging from less than £50 to £25,000. Lily May Johnson bequeathed £13,393, Hilda Dearden £22,500, and Beryl Clarebrough (as a memorial to her sister Phyllis Clarebrough) £25,000.

Resignations, for a variety of reasons including old age and moving away from the locality, also brought about a change in the Presidency, Chairmanship and composition of the Executive Committee. It was announced at the Executive Meeting in June 1986 that Sir Eric Mensforth, who was leaving Sheffield to live in Epsom, had decided that he must resign the Presidency after eleven years. The Annual Report for 1987 said he had given the Branch 'unstintingly of his time and influence in pursuing our objectives'. General Sir Hugh Beach, a member of the Branch for 22 years and with a family estate in the Peak Park, accepted the invitation to be the next President.

Resignations of other Executive Committee members included Frank Colley in 1990; he had been a member of the Executive Committee since 1963. Arthur Humphrey gave up the position of Assistant Treasurer in 1989 on reaching his 80th birthday but remained an Executive Committee member until 1993. Then in 1992, George Shaw relinquished the Chairmanship (but remained on the Executive Committee) upon his appointment to the Peak Park Joint Planning Board and was succeeded by Andrew Shepherd, an architect in private practice and Chairman of the Hallamshire Historic Buildings Society.

After the departure of Lynn Crowe in 1985, Elizabeth Garland was appointed as Assistant Technical Officer, the title being changed to Technical Secretary by 1991, a reflection of her increasing responsibility and the faith put in her by Gerald. She took the helm quickly, greatly relieved the burden on Gerald, and dealt with technical matters with great aplomb and authority. It was a great loss to the Branch when she left in the spring of 1993 to become Director of the Association for the Protection of Rural Scotland. Her former Technical Assistant, Tim Richardson, who had been appointed early in 1991, succeeded her as Technical Secretary in April

1993, but he left in less than a year. He was succeeded in May 1994 by Dennis Patton, who came to the Branch following a varied career in the public and voluntary sector with Sheffield City Council, Greenpeace, the Royal Society for Nature Conservation and the British Trust for Conservation Volunteers. Kim Wilson was appointed as Planning Officer in April 1993 but she resigned in late 1994 and was replaced by David Bradley, who had taken early retirement from Sheffield City Council, where he had been Assistant Environmental Planning Officer.

Among all this chopping and changing in the early 1990s, there was, besides Gerald, one other pillar of stability and continuity: Jean Smart. Jean who had first come to work in the Branch office in 1963, celebrated thirty years in post in 1993. In 1990 the name of her post had been changed from Assistant Secretary to Administrative Secretary, to more fully reflect her seniority and wide-ranging role. Margaret Gray joined Jean in the office in June 1992 as Secretarial Assistant.

Gerald with Jean Smart at the tree planting ceremony at Dore in November 1994 of the first trees in the Haythornthwaite Memorial Woodland.

Another event that ensured stability, this time for the future, was Gerald's announcement at the Executive Meeting held in March 1989 that although he had agreed to sell 22 Endcliffe Crescent to the University of Sheffield in the event of his wishing to sell, or his death, the university had agreed that it had no objections to the handing over of the outbuildings to the Branch by Gerald by deed of gift. The result would be that the Branch would own its offices, garage, outbuildings and curtilage. The Executive Committee was asked by Gerald to approve the arrangement which it did 'with acclamation'. It was reported at the Executive Committee meeting in October 1989 that the deed of gift had been completed.

A further momentous event was the decision to enlarge the area for which the Branch was responsible to include Barnsley and Doncaster Metropolitan Districts, thus covering the whole of South Yorkshire. The issue was first raised at the Executive Meeting in July 1990. It was reported that the South and West Yorkshire branch of the CPRE had ceased to operate and the National Office had asked the Branch to take on the areas formerly covered by them. The first thing that was agreed was that if the Branch took responsibility for Barnsley and Doncaster Metropolitan

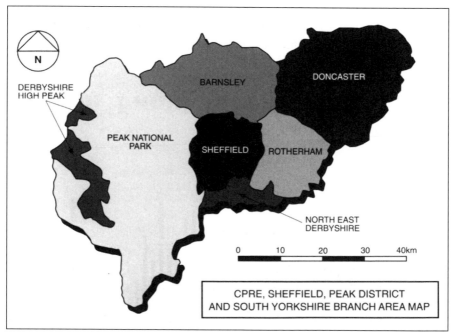

The area covered by the Branch after incorporating Barnsley and Doncaster Metropolitan Districts.

Districts, there should not be any change of name for the Branch unless it were to add the words 'with South Yorkshire'. Elizabeth Garland made the point that for the purposes of the unitary development plan, South Yorkshire was one unit. It would be difficult, she pointed out, to deal with Sheffield and Rotherham in isolation from the other two metropolitan districts. She was of the firm opinion that one branch of CPRE should be dealing with the whole of South Yorkshire. The Chairman wondered if the staff would be able to cope with the extra work involved. It was argued that an extra member of staff would be required and it was suggested that the National Office might provide funding. Arthur Humphrey was in favour of expansion and thought the Branch could afford the added expenditure. Gerald was lukewarm to the proposal and was of the opinion that the office was in full use already. After a long discussion it was decided to accede to the request but to look for some funding from the National Office. At the July 1990 Executive Meeting Gerald confirmed that the Branch had agreed with London to incorporate the rest of South Yorkshire within its operational boundaries, but again stressed this would place a strain on resources and that some selectivity would have to made in the issues taken up in the new areas. Tim Richardson, as already noted, was appointed as Technical Assistant early in 1991 to help cope with the extra workload and the official change of name—CPRE, Sheffield, Peak District and South Yorkshire Branch—occurred at the Annual General Meeting in May that year. The area of operations then covered 900 square miles, 'from the peatbogs of Thorne Moors to Buxton's limestone quarries' as the 1992 Annual Report put it.

In 1992 a support group was established in Rotherham which from the outset played a valuable role in scrutinising planning lists, commenting on planning documents and providing information for public inquiries.

II

Not until almost the end of the 1980s was a final resolution arrived at in the strained relationship with the London Office (Gerald avoided the use of the term 'Headquarters'!) over the issue of centralisation of membership and records and contributions from branches into national funds. It was the first substantive item on the agenda at the March 1985 Executive Meeting. At that meeting Gerald outlined once again the longstanding objections of the Branch to the national organisation's desire to centralise membership subscriptions and records as detailed most recently in the proposals for a development plan and revised membership structure due to be considered by the National Executive Committee in June 1985. In a note that had been circulated to all members of the Executive Committee in advance of the March meeting, he emphasised that the proposals

> *would seriously debilitate the Branch by interfering with direct communication with our members and by reducing the income from membership subscriptions and also reducing the likelihood of receiving legacies which have sustained us in the past.*

He went on in his note to state that the Director of CPRE, Robin Grove-White, had written to the Branch expressing his disquiet that the Branch Executive Committee had not asked either himself or Chairman David Astor to discuss the CPRE's development plan/membership structure with them. Gerald reminded members of the Executive Committee that they had explained their objections in previous correspondence and it was considered that 'there would be no benefit in further personal discussions.'

At the meeting Gerald underlined his argument in the note, emphasising the loss of independence both operationally and financially that the Branch would suffer if it acceded to the London Office's proposals. The Committee agreed that there had been no change of position of the Branch in relation to the London Office and that they should pursue the course they had already set themselves. It was also agreed to support the Exmoor Society's proposed amendment to CPRE membership which suggested that those county branches which had decided, in accordance with their constitutions, to retain their own membership, publications and subscriptions, should be able to opt for affiliation or county association status (or its equivalent in the cases of those branches covering more than one county). It was also agreed to send a polite reply to the request for discussions about the whole issue and to suggest to the London Office that in future the Branch should call itself 'Council for the Protection of Rural England for Sheffield and the Peak District'.

In July it was reported to the Executive Committee that the national development plan/membership structure paper had been adopted by Council at the June meeting. It was agreed to send the usual contribution to the national funds and to wait for a further communication from the London Office. In September it was reported that Council had rejected the Exmoor Society's proposal concerning county association status, and the London Office had asked when the Branch intended to join the computerised membership administration system. Gerald reported that he had replied, stating that the Branch did not intend to join the system in the foreseeable future. The Executive Committee took note and approved. Further disagreement with the national organisation took place in the spring of 1986 when it was reported that the London Office wished to approach parish councils and other affiliated organisations in the Branch's area to invite them to become national members. At that time the Branch had 65 affiliated organisations in its membership, including fifteen parish councils. The Committee agreed that it did not wish its affiliated organisations to be approached for this purpose as it was felt it would cause confusion and lead to a loss of members.

The next major development took place in the summer of 1987 when at the July Executive Committee meeting, Chairman George Shaw outlined the three alternatives facing the Branch in the light of the new national constitution. It could remain a Branch, which would mean joining fully in the membership structure scheme but retaining a large degree of autonomy; or it could become a county association which would mean that its autonomy would be retained but would result in reduced national voting rights and possibly losing the CPRE banner; or it could break away from CPRE entirely. There was then a long discussion in which the advantages of belonging to an increasingly effective national organisation, the importance of the words 'Council for the Protection of Rural England' in the Branch's identity, and the success of the Branch as a local organisation with local supporters, were batted back and forth. In the end it was decided to set up a sub-committee to make further investigations and to make recommendations to the next meeting of the Executive Committee. At the September Executive Committee meeting the sub-committee recommended that the request for county association status should be re-affirmed, and this was agreed as was the contents of a letter to the new National Director, Andrew Purkis. The letter emphasised that the Branch wished to remain publicly associated with CPRE and to retain 'Council for the Protection of Rural England' in letter headings and publications, but for the reasons that were again explained at length, circumstances required that 'we should be an independent body both financially and operationally, acting as an Association of the C.P.R.E.' The letter ended by suggesting that an appropriate new title for the Branch would be 'Council for the Protection of Rural England, Sheffield and Peak District Association'.

The reaction to the letter in the London Office was that Andrew Purkis asked for a discussion with the officers of the Branch before a final decision was taken. A meeting with the sub-committee appointed to make recommendations about the future status of the Branch took place on 16 October. The National Director clarified the position and obviously made a big impression on those he met. First of all he emphasised that the Sheffield and Peak District Branch was regarded as a 'special' and 'very important' Branch of the CPRE. The only change he saw from the present position in remaining a branch related to terms of membership. He also pointed out that if the Branch opted for county association status, its members would no longer be members of the CPRE. He also considered it unlikely that other branches would agree to the use of the CPRE name if it was no longer a branch. Gerald told the rest of the Executive Committee at the November meeting that the use of the CPRE name was vital. He therefore considered that the correct course of action was for them to remain a branch. Derek Grayson and Arthur Humphrey also both said they found it difficult to maintain their opposition to remaining a branch after having heard the case put by Andrew Purkis. After further discussion it was proposed that the application for county association status be withdrawn, and that the Branch should remain a branch under the new centralised membership system. The proposal was carried with one member voting against it.

The decision was presented to the Annual General Meeting on 30 April 1988 and passed with one member voting against. The Branch rules were changed to take on board the new membership system and the new rules were approved by the London Office in December 1988 and by the Charities Commission early in 1989.

III

In presenting the Annual Report at the Annual General Meeting in May 1989, George Shaw said that when he became Chairman at the beginning of the 1980s, the Branch's main concern had been the establishment of the three green belts of Rotherham, Sheffield and North East Derbyshire. 'We hoped', he went on, 'that once these were established, together with the protection of the National Park, the future of our countryside was assured. This has not proved to be the case.' Indeed, demands on green belt land for housing, for commercial and industrial development, and for venues for leisure and recreation in the area covered by the Branch (including, of course, the extension of that area to include the whole of South Yorkshire) remained at a high level throughout the period from 1986 to 1995 and put extreme pressure on the Branch's technical, administrative and secretarial staff.

Proposals for housing development were objected to at various places to the east of Sheffield and Rotherham, near to the M1 and M18 motorways. In 1985 the Branch objected, along with many local residents, to the proposed development of Spenn's Field at Harthill, as part of the Harthill/ Woodsetts District Plan, on the grounds that the development would be detrimental to the scale and character of the village. A public inquiry took place in October that year and the inspector recommended that the site should not be built upon and that it should be included in the Rotherham Green Belt. This recommendation was put to Rotherham Council for its approval, but was defeated by 50 votes to five. The Branch decided to continue to press for its inclusion in the Green Belt. In 1990 a proposed residential development at Sandy Lane, Bramley was refused on appeal on the grounds of prematurity in terms of the Unitary Development Plan and because of the grade of the agricultural land.

The largest proposal for development in Sheffield's Green Belt came in 1986 when Henry Boot Homes Ltd proposed to build 120,000 square feet of retail space, 320 houses, and a medical centre, with related infor-mal recreation areas and parking for 1,000 cars in Oakes Park at Norton. The site was not only within the Green Belt, but also in a conservation area with listed buildings. A public inquiry was held in September 1988 at which Elizabeth Garland presented the Branch's case. The appeal by the developer was dismissed.

In the Sheffield Green Belt the most interesting case concerned a pro-posed residential development off Skew Hill, Grenoside, the twelve-acre site being one which had been developed in the Second World War as a Ministry of Defence munitions depot. It was argued by the developer that the site had already been developed for light industry. At the public inquiry, held in June 1990, the inspector dismissed the appeal and ruled that if the proposal had been permitted it would have resulted in the intensification of development and a suburbanisation of the site's appearance. Furthermore, he concluded, it would have resulted in the replacement of one form of inappropriate develop-ment in the Green Belt with another. The decision was not only approved of by the Executive Committee but the underlying arguments by the inspector were seen as very important principles to record for use in the future.

In 1991 the Branch played a large part in the vigorous objections to the development of a 'model village' in the Sheffield Green Belt at Totley. The site was bounded by the A621 Baslow Road, Totley Hall Lane and the then Sheffield City Polytechnic campus. The application sought approval for 180 residential units, a golf course, information centre, restaurant, public house, and church, the whole development covering about 50 acres. Elizabeth Garland addressed the City Council's Planning Committee on behalf of not only the Branch but also Totley Residents' Association. About 150 Totley residents attended the meeting. The proposal was rejected unanimously by the Planning Committee.

There were also worrying applications for industrial development in areas within local green belts. Quarrying applications, for example were not restricted to the White Peak. In 1993 the Branch submitted written objections to a public inquiry concerned with a controversial proposal to quarry Magnesian Limestone from a 134-acre greenfield site west of Campsall in Doncaster Metropolitan District. The quarrying was planned to extend over eighteen years. The proposal was turned down not only because of the damage it would do to the countryside, but also because of alternative sources of supply.

The trend towards out of town shopping centres and office parks was reflected by two worrying proposals at sites on green belt land, one partly in Sheffield and North East Derbyshire and the other in Rotherham. In 1985 Asda Stores proposed to build a superstore with parking for 750 cars on the site of the former RAF station at Norton straddling the Sheffield and North East Derbyshire boundary. Asda approached the Branch and asked for support for their proposal; in return Asda Stores offered to tidy up the remainder of the area. The Branch was, of course, implacably opposed to the proposal. Both local authorities refused planning permission and a public inquiry was planned to take place in January 1986. Asda Stores then withdrew its appeal and the scheme was dropped. In neighbouring Rotherham in 1988 a proposal was made for a 'hi-tech' business and science park on green belt land at Whiston Meadows. The appeal was dismissed.

The water industry submitted a number of applications for treatment works in Sheffield's Green Belt to the west of the city to which the Branch objected. The Branch presented its objections to Yorkshire Water Authority's proposal to erect 83,000 square feet of buildings and a covered reservoir between Wharncliffe Side and Brightholmlee conservation area, and within a quarter of a mile of the boundary of the Peak Park. The Water Authority based its proposal on the necessity to comply with EEC regulations. The Branch did not think other sites had been adequately considered. The proposal was also opposed by a strong local residents' action group and the local parish council. A public inquiry was held in May 1988, with the Branch's case being presented by John Fox, a member of the Executive Committee. The appeal against the refusal of planning permission was dismissed. This proposal was soon followed by others. In 1989 there were proposals for treatment works at Stacey Bank Farm in the Loxley Valley and Trouble Wood, Bradfield, both in extremely exposed positions, the first in the Sheffield Green Belt and the second in the Peak Park. These were followed in 1990 with proposals for such works at Storrs Bridge in the Loxley Valley and at Ewden (to replace the site at Brightholmlee turned down in 1988).

Opposing proposals for hotel developments with or without related leisure attractions on sites within green belts also occupied a substantial amount of time in this period. An application for the erection of a 150 bedroom hotel with restaurant and leisure and conference facilities by Scottish and Newcastle Breweries in the Rotherham Green Belt near junction 31 of the M1 at Aston was approved following a week-long public inquiry in April 1989. Rotherham Borough Council did not oppose the scheme. However, the application was called in by the new Secretary of State who dismissed the appeal in December 1989. In December 1993 there was a five-day public inquiry into the proposal to build a hotel, restaurant and petrol station on green belt land near junction 33 of the M1 at Catcliffe. Again the application was approved by Rotherham Borough Council. The 1995 Annual Report described the public inquiry as 'a bruising experience'. The appeal was approved.

The period also saw the proposal of a number of leisure and recreation developments that would have had a marked effect on the character of sites on green belt land. In November 1987 Elizabeth Garland presented the Branch's objections to a proposal for two dry ski slopes and related buildings at The Reaps, Rivelin Valley Road, Sheffield. In recommending dismissal of the appeal, the inspector said the development 'would make an irrevocable

Tree felling for hotel building at the foot of Canklow Wood. The proposal for associated dry ski slopes did not proceed. (Joan Jones)

change to the landscape'. A potentially more damaging ski slope scheme was put forward in 1987 in Canklow Wood in Rotherham, an ancient wood containing an important Iron Age archaeological site that surveys had shown survived within the proposed development area. The proposal was given approval by Rotherham Borough Council's Planning Committee by the casting vote of the Chairman. A site meeting subsequently took place at which Elizabeth Garland, the Duke of Norfolk's agent (the Duke was the owner of the site), the developer, and representatives of English Heritage, the Nature Conservancy Council and South Yorkshire Archaeological Unit were present. Evidence that the archaeological site extended from the Scheduled Ancient Monument at the top of the slope down through the wood where the two parallel dry ski slopes were planned had been sent to the Duke's agent. At that point a lease had not been signed. In the light of the archaeological evidence the Duke agreed that 'for the time being' there would be no ski slope development. The application was then withdrawn.

Golf course proposals also threatened large-scale land use change in the green belt. In 1991 the Branch expressed its concern to Doncaster Metropolitan District Council over an application for a golf course and new village on 830 hectares (2,000 acres) of land south and west of Rossington, together with a new link road to the M18. Doncaster MBC ruled that the proposal was premature because the Unitary Development Plan was in preparation. In August 1992 the Branch presented its objections at a public inquiry concerning an application to build a hotel on land at Hollin Berry Farm at Howbrook between Sheffield and Barnsley. The appeal was turned down. In his decision letter the inspector stated that the proposed development would prejudice the objectives of green belt designation and result in significant harm to the character and appearance of the area. Within a short period of time there was another proposal for the same area to remove coal by opencast methods on a 120 acre site and to build a golf course on the landscaped site. A public inquiry took place in March 1995 and the appeal was dismissed.

The Branch was also involved in the second half of the 1980s and early 1990s with a number of campaigns concerned with woodlands and the agricultural character of green belt areas. For example, at the September 1985 Executive Committee Meeting it was reported that work had begun, by Sheffield City Council's Recreation Department, upon a ten-year management plan in the woods at Acorn Hill in the Loxley Valley. It had been agreed that the public would be informed about the plan before work began, but this had not happened, and the work had caused a great deal of concern to local people. The outcry was such, including assertions of 'Council vandalism', that work was suspended. By the spring of 1986,

Controversial woodland management in Little Matlock Wood at Acorn Hill in the Loxley Valley in 1985–1986. (Joan Jones)

following a site visit by the Moorlands and Amenity Woodlands Advisory Group, attended by Elizabeth Garland, and a public meeting organised by the Loxley Valley Protection Society, a number of amendments were made to the management plan, most notably the extension of the cycle of sycamore removal, and it was agreed that the public and local societies, including CPRE, would be kept informed of work schedules in future. The Acorn Hill incident was important in that it led to a much more strategic approach to woodland management in the city, enshrined within two years in a woodland policy document.

Hedgerows had also come under threat in the eastern half of South Yorkshire. During 1991 the Branch was active in support of CPRE's national campaign promoting the introduction of new legislation to protect hedges. A new hedgerow management grant scheme resulted and the Government promised additional protective legislation. Locally, the Branch launched a hedgerow survey scheme in Rotherham during Environment Week in May 1991 and in July that year the Branch stated its concern over the Dun Drainage Commission's drainage scheme which would have a marked effect on the enclosed and atmospheric historic landscape of the Fishlake area, unique in South Yorkshire, with its network of winding lanes, pastures

Hedged landscape, Letwell. (Jim Flanagan)

and meadows in hedged fields, mature roadside and hedgerow oaks, ashes and willows, and farm ponds.

In addition to the detailed casework and campaigning, the technical staff in the second half of the 1980s and first half of the 1990s were also concerned with more general local issues in the form of the Rotherham and Barnsley Green Belt plans, Unitary Development Plans (UDPs) for Sheffield, Rotherham, Barnsley and Doncaster, and the Local Plan for North East Derbyshire.

The inquiry into the Rotherham Green Belt Plan was held in January 1988 and Elizabeth Garland presented evidence in support of the Branch's objections to the proposed deletion from the green belt land of sites at Ravenfield Common, Aston, Fence, Swallownest and Spenn's Field at Harthill. However, major modifications were proposed by the Borough Council at Whiston and Bramley in order to accommodate 'hi tech' development and this led to a further public inquiry in November 1989. The inspector's report recommended refusal, noting that he recognised the Borough's need for such development but felt it could be accommodated on reclaimed industrial land within the town. The Borough Council agreed to accept the inspector's report, and the plan was approved by the Secretary of State in June 1990.

The Branch was very concerned in 1990, in advance of the preparation of their UDP, that Barnsley Metropolitan Council was proposing to remove seven sites around the M1 from their Green Belt. When the Deposit version of the UDP was published in November 1994, although there were copious references to sustainable development, the proposals still contained a substantial number of releases of green belt land for industrial development in the M1 corridor. The Branch considered that as these sites would be very attractive to investors and businesses, they would undermine the Council's proposals for regenerating declining coalfield communities. Deep concern was also expressed when the first draft of the Doncaster UDP was received in December 1992. It was seen as very much a development-led plan 'which would have a devastating effect on the local countryside'. Although the Branch submitted a number of objections to the Sheffield UDP in 1993, it was pleased with the 'negotiating process' adopted by the Sheffield planners, which would, it was hoped, lead to much more productive use of expensive public inquiry time, when the inquiry took place in March 1995. The Branch made 23 representations on the draft Local Plan for North East Derbyshire in 1995, but was in general support of the policies in the plan that consolidated the Green Belt there and conserved the historic countryside and its many traditional buildings.

IV

In the Peak Park in this period, concerns ranged as widely as they had ever done, but as in the past the impact of quarrying and related industrial development overshadowed all other concerns. The period began with two important public inquiries related to Tarmac Roadstone's Topley Pike Quarry and T.W. Ward Roadstone's Eldon Hill Quarry. The Topley Pike Quarry inquiry took place in April 1985 and Gerald gave evidence on behalf of the Branch and the Voluntary Joint Committee and appeared as a witness for the Council for National Parks. The appeal was dismissed with the inspector concluding that the extension would be a threat to the natural beauty and attractiveness of the area and that there was no clear need to extend the site. The inquiry about Eldon Hill, held in Buxton, began in late November 1985 and went on until the end of January 1986. Elizabeth Garland, in Gerald's enforced absence, led the case on behalf of the Branch and the Voluntary Joint Committee, attending on fourteen days, on some occasions in atrocious snowy weather which led to long, circuitous rail journeys via Manchester. But the effort was worthwhile: the appeal to extend the quarry was dismissed and the end to one of the longest campaigns the Branch had fought, extending back into the late 1930s, was in sight at last.

There were, of course, other threats in other locations. In December 1985, for example, Laporte Industries proposed to extract fluorspar at Mill Dam Mine, Great Hucklow. It was reported at the December 1985 Executive Committee meeting that this had been objected to because the site was very near the village and there would be much disturbance, dust and noise and a new link road would have to be built. At the March 1986 Executive Meeting it was reported that the Peak Park Planning Board had granted permission to the development subject to 48 conditions. In 1987 it became known that Blue Circle intended to apply to divert Castleton Lane at the Hope Cement Works in order to open up a large area of limestone which was of better quality than on their existing permissions and the working of which would result in the long run in a well landscaped dale, although there would be an exposed cliff visible for many miles around during the working period. There was a long discussion about the application at the Executive meeting in March 1988, in particular about the short term and long term implications. It was finally decided to oppose the alteration, but the proposal was subsequently approved by the Peak Park Planning Board. In 1991 the Branch objected to the proposed extension of Darlton Quarry at Stoney Middleton, based on the lack of national need, the availability of alternative sources and the effect of the development on heavy traffic in the White Peak. There was deep disappointment that the Peak Park Joint Planning Board granted permission even though it imposed a strict life span and severe environmental conditions. Right at the end of the period, Eldon Hill came onto the agenda again when the owners applied to extend the termination date for the quarry set by the Minister 44 years earlier. The Peak Park Board turned down the application.

On the industrial front, the Branch objected to a number of industrial developments that were out of character with the areas in which they were set. In 1987, for example, the Branch took exception both to the fact that the scrap metal yard at Hathersage Station (said to be the third largest stainless steel scrap metal yard in the country) had expanded beyond the area for which the owner had been granted planning permission and that it was suspected that the Peak Park Planning Board was likely to grant retrospective permission for the unauthorised areas. Meetings were held with local residents and a site meeting took place in July 1987. Planning permission was granted with conditions, the Branch being involved in the setting of conditions. In the same year the Branch objected strongly to the proposal to build a 'hi tech' factory on Haddon Road in Bakewell with parking for 100 vehicles. The proposal was contrary to the Peak Park Structure Plan and in Gerald's opinion would grossly disfigure the approaches to Bakewell from Haddon Hall. Permission was refused by the Peak Park Board. Also in 1987, Carbolite of Bamford Mill, furnace makers, applied to construct a new factory on land adjoining Hope Station and the Branch objected because of the openness of the site, the precedent that would be set for other firms wanting to locate along the railway line, and the deviation which the application set from the Park Structure Plan (it was outside an existing settlement). The Board advertised the application as a departure from the Structure Plan but the Secretary of State decided not to call in the application and it was left to the Board to make a final decision. The Board approved the application, the fact that 100 jobs were involved being an important deciding factor.

The Branch was also concerned with proposed new uses for surviving old industrial buildings. At the October 1988 Executive Committee meeting it was reported that it was proposed to convert Litton Mill, near Tideswell into a timeshare development although a planning application had not yet been submitted. Discussion covered issues such as traffic that would be generated, the preference for residential conversion to homes for local residents, and concern in some quarters of the fate of the building if the development was not allowed. The mill was subsequently sold to another development company which submitted another application that came before the Peak Park Planning Board in July 1989. The plan proposed the conversion of Litton Mill into a hotel and to provide 55 timeshare apartments within the site. This was seen by CPRE supporters as 'suburbanisation of the countryside'. In the meantime the Litton Mill Community Group had gathered a petition of 14,000 signatories against the timeshare proposals. The application was turned down. The developer appealed and a public inquiry took place on fourteen days over a six week period in 1991 with Elizabeth Garland giving evidence on behalf of the Branch and for the Council for National Parks. The appeal was dismissed. The case was repeated almost identically in 1990 and 1991 at Cressbrook Mill where there was a proposal to convert the premises into a mixed development of offices and residential and holiday accommodation. The Branch objected to the over-development of the site, the amount of new building and difficulties of access along a narrow road. The application was refused by the Peak Park Planning Board.

Other proposed recreation/tourism developments that brought opposition from the Branch included the use of Holly Bank Quarry, Tintwistle, as a rifle range (refused on appeal, 1988); the development of a water sports centre at

Litton Mill.

Bottoms Reservoir, Tintwistle (refused by Peak Park Planning Board, 1988; appeal lodged and then withdrawn, then another application threatened); and extended parking and new visitor facilities at Heatherdene by Severn Trent Water on the shores of Ladybower Reservoir, which in the view of the Branch was in danger of being over-developed (application refused, 1994).

An important campaign in relation to farm buildings was finally won in 1990 when the Peak Park Planning Board, after more than two decades of lobbying from the Branch, finally agreed that factory coloured sheeting for farm buildings should be specified for all new farm buildings. Promises in the past to have sheets painted after construction had often remained unfulfilled.

V

Gerald died on 4 January 1995, 59 years, almost to the day, after starting work for the Branch on 2 January 1936. He was 82.

Following his death tributes flowed in from all quarters. Jonathan Dimbleby, then National President of the CPRE, said he was 'a remarkable

Lt. Col. Gerald Haythornthwaite, CBE, TD, FRIBA, FRTPI, 1912–1995.

figure…a pioneer with a persuasive and thoughtful influence'. The National Chairman of the CPRE, Lord Marlesford, said he was 'a unique and dedicated champion of the countryside, whose reputation and influence are unparalleled by anyone today'. James Turner of the National Trust, East Midlands Region, said 'he was so often a guiding light for us as well as the CPRE' and Margaret Davey of the Dartmoor Preservation Association also stressed his influence beyond South Yorkshire and the Peak District, writing that his work 'set an example which encouraged others wherever they lived. He will certainly not be forgotten here'. At his memorial service Fiona Reynolds, National Director of the CPRE, spoke of 'his enormous zest for the task' and his tirelessness and dauntless approach in the face of 'seemingly insurmountable obstacles'.

Nearer to home, Andrew Shepherd referred to Gerald in the 1995 Annual Report as 'the benign sage'. In responding to letters from far and wide which often linked the contribution of Gerald with that of Ethel, he said he was 'surprised at the extent of the spread of their influence and that it was so fondly remembered.' Roy Bullen, who knew Gerald not only through membership of the Executive Committee but also through expeditions into the Peak District with volunteers to do practical conservation work, remembered him as a caring encourager of others, as a brilliant publicist for the conservationist cause, and as someone who never or rarely lost his temper whatever the provocation. For Jean Smart, who worked very closely with Gerald for more than thirty years, it was the combination of meticulous preparation, reasoned argument and realistic alternatives that marked Gerald out as the consummate professional. For Jack Burling, it was Gerald's level of preparation and grasp of technical detail at public inquiries, that left Jack gasping and in awe.

Gerald died as he was preparing for another working day in the job he loved. But he almost didn't take the job. Many years after coming to Sheffield for interview in November 1935, he recalled his first impressions of Sheffield as he emerged from the railway station:

> *I stood at the exit. There was a pall of sooty smoke over everything, and I thought 'I'm going home'. Even by Bolton standards, it looked a thoroughly unpleasant place to live in.*

He changed his mind. And it is no exaggeration to say he changed people's lives.

10

Postscript:
Celebrating the past and shaping the future

RESEARCHING AND WRITING the history of the CPRE, Sheffield, Peak District and South Yorkshire Branch has been a privileged journey into the past, into the history of the countryside conservation movement, and into the most recent stages of the landscape history of the Peak District and South Yorkshire. And whatever sources have been poured over—the formal minutes of more than 70 years of committee meetings, annual reports (there has been one every year since 1931, and the first one covered the period from 1924 to 1931), press coverage, or private papers and private correspondence—the same ethos emerges: *sharp focus*, *high principles*, unwaveringly adhered to; and, with the passage of time, that great advantage for local campaigners, *continuity*, accumulating, as it stretched on and on, experience, precedent, memory—and legacies. In evaluating the contribution of the Branch to countryside conservation, it is worth considering each of these characteristics in turn.

With relatively few notable exceptions, for example, Gerald's involvement with the North Wales campaign against the establishment of a nuclear power station there, or the Executive Committee's lobbying of a succession of central governments to adopt for every national park the planning board structure and composition operating in the Peak Park, the Branch has always been sharply focused on local issues. This was most cogently and tellingly expressed in the letter sent to the London Office in December 1975 in response to moves to centralise membership and subscriptions. It was local interest that maintained the Branch, the letter pointed out. There was an intimate relationship between the Branch office and its members, which was an essential element of the Branch's vitality. Most members joined not because of a general interest in the planning of the countryside, but because of interest in the local countryside, and often just for a particular part of it.

That sharp focus has always been allied to an unerring ability to cover every conceivable issue of local importance, and to draw attention to matters of concern that apparently had not even appeared on the agendas of the appropriate authorities. And mastery of the technical details and legal niceties has been a characteristic of the Branch's work from the very beginning, either through the sheer hard work by the Branch's officers and Executive Committee members or through the ability of Ethel and Gerald to bring on board appropriate experts from the local area or from much further afield.

The work of the Branch has also been based on clear-cut principles from the very outset. Principles upheld by the most thorough preparation and rational argument. As Gerald told Stephen McClarence in an interview published in *The Star* in 1987: 'sensible argument is the right way—and getting your facts right. We enter the lists through public enquiries. We don't go in for bombing places.' The Branch has not gone in for compromise either, or retreating from tough decisions, or ducking unpopularity in high places. Neither did Gerald and Ethel shrink from telling people politely but directly that giving way in part, however small that part, was the beginning of the end, the thin end of the wedge; 'trimming' was not their way of life.

The Branch's stance, solid and unyielding through more than three-quarters of a century stands in great contrast to that of the local authorities whose areas corresponded with those of the Branch. Their planning history is, it must be said, one peppered with ineptitude, bad judgement, lack of imagination, broken promises and short-termism, as the preceding nine chapters have clearly shown. Only the Peak Park Planning Board emerges with a glowing reputation.

One shudders to think what the Peak District would look like at the beginning of the twenty-first century if the Branch had not existed for a quarter of a century before the creation of the Peak Park and its Planning Board: ubiquitous spoliation of the White Peak through quarrying; wide, multiple-lane motor roads cutting through former remote areas; sub-urbanisation of the landscape everywhere in inappropriate styles and materials; intrusive and gaudy advertising at every turn; the place turned into a fairground by uncontrolled recreational developments; the region's traditional character almost submerged. And a similar litany of inappropriate developments could be listed for what is now green belt land in South Yorkshire, the battle against which was more protracted than in the Peak. Some campaigns were lost in both arenas, but many notable ones were won and thinking about landscape protection was fundamentally changed.

Ethel and Gerald at the helm covered, between them, 71 years. In that time, central governments, secretaries of state, local politicians, local planning officials, executives of private companies, newspaper owners and editors, chairmen and directors of the CPRE national organisation, came and went, time and time again. Ethel and Gerald went on. Experience and expertise increased, memory lengthened. Setbacks were accommodated but they never caused any deviation from their 'grand purposes'.

Times have changed, and Ethel and Gerald have both gone. But the Branch continues on its way into the twenty-first century. So what of the future? There are new issues, for example, the future of the upland farmer and the possible impact on the Peak District landscape; economic regeneration programmes and landscape conservation in South Yorkshire. And there are many perennial ones including road transport planning, quarrying, hedgerow removal, and housing proposals on greenfield sites.

The possible impact of these and other threats to the countryside in the Peak District and South Yorkshire will continue to be monitored by scrutinising planning applications and influencing decisions within the planning system. And as in the past, a watchful eye will be kept on the 'bigger picture': strategic plans, and central government and European policies as they affect the local countryside will be kept under constant review and representations made as appropriate.

Offering advice to local community groups will remain an important priority for the future. And this is likely to reap its own rewards as in the past, in the recruitment of new members and supporters. Local links have always been crucial and will remain so. The kind of unpaid commitment given by Gerald and Ethel is a thing of the past and can never be repeated. Administrative and technical expertise must be paid for, and the work of an enlarged band of volunteers, co-ordinated by the Branch's planning officer and others is likely to be a key ingredient in the mix of future Branch activity.

In a time of growing environmental awareness and concern, but also one of unprecedented affluence and material selfishness, the role of the Branch as a consciousness raiser is likely to be a critical one, not only in terms of protecting the countryside, but also in continuing to make its own presence known and its successful campaigning record recognised among new generations.

There is now a closer relationship with the National Office than in earlier years, but the Branch is still determined to keep its financial and operational independence and continue to use its now substantial resources to fight local issues to protect the countryside in the surrounding region, continuing the vision of the Haythornthwaites with the same vigour as before into the new century.

Friends *of the*
Peak District

CPRE Sheffield, Peak District and South Yorkshire Branch continues to campaign for the protection of the local countryside. Membership is open to all.

If you would like to help with our work or if you would simply like more information, please contact us at:

'The Stables'
22a Endcliffe Crescent
Sheffield S10 3EF

Tel: 0114 266 5822; Fax: 0114 268 5510
E-mail: info@cprepeakandsyorks.org.uk

Registered Charity No. 227429

Index